DATE DUE

NOV 26 2005			

A TRAVEL GUIDE TO
Al Capone's
Chicago

A TRAVEL GUIDE TO
Al Capone's
Chicago

Other books in the Travel Guide series:

Ancient Alexandria
Ancient Athens
Ancient Rome
Medieval Constantinople
Renaissance Florence
Shakespeare's London

Diane Yancey

San Diego • Detroit • New York • San Francisco • Cleveland • New Haven, Conn. • Waterville, Maine • London • Munich

For more information, contact
Lucent Books
27500 Drake Rd.
Farmington Hills, MI 48331-3535
Or you can visit our Internet site at http://www.gale.com.

LIBRARY OF CONGRESS CATALOGING-IN-PUBLICATION DATA

Yancey, Diane.
Al Capone's Chicago / by Diane Yancey.
p. cm. — (A travel guide to:)
Summary: Describes what a visitor to Chicago in 1929 would find to see and do, including providing references to famous gangster activities and haunts.
Includes bibliographical references and index.
ISBN 1-59018-248-0 (lib. bdg. : alk. paper)
1. Chicago (Ill.)—History—1875—Juvenile literature. 2. Chicago (Ill.)—Description and travel—Juvenile literature. 3. Chicago (Ill.)—Social life and customs—20th century—Juvenile literature. 4. Capone, Al, 1899–1947—Homes and haunts—Illinois—Chicago—Juvenile literature. 5. Gangsters—Illinois—Chicago—History—20th century—Juvenile literature. [1. Chicago (Ill.)—History—1875–2. Chicago (Ill.)—Social life and customs—20th century. 3. Gangsters.] I. Title. II. Series.
F548.5 .Y36 2003
977.3'11—dc21

2002013976

Printed in the United States of America

Contents

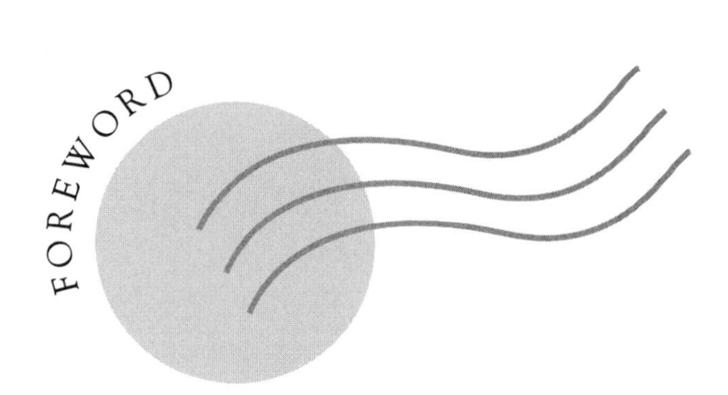

Travel can be a unique way to learn about oneself and other cultures. The esteemed American writer and historian John Hope Franklin poetically expressed his conviction in the value of travel by urging, "We must go beyond textbooks, go out into the bypaths and untrodden depths of the wilderness and travel and explore and tell the world the glories of our journey." The message communicated by this eloquent entreaty is clear: The value of travel is to temper one's imagination about a place and its people with reality, and instead of thinking how things may be, to be able to experience them as they really are.

Franklin's voice is not alone in his summons for students to "travel and explore." He is joined by a stentorian chorus of thinkers that includes former president John F. Kennedy, who established the Peace Corps to facilitate cross-cultural understandings between Americans and citizens of other lands. Ideas about the benefits of travel do not spring only from contemporary times. The ancient Greek historian Herodotus journeyed to foreign lands for the purpose of immersing himself in unfamiliar cultural traditions. In this way, he believed, he might gain a firsthand understanding of people and ways of life in other places.

The joys, insights, and satisfaction that travelers derive from their journeys are not limited to cultural understanding. Travel has the added value of enhancing the traveler's inner self by expanding his or her range of experiences. Writer Paul Tournier concurs that, "The real meaning of travel, like that of a conversation by the fireside, is the discovery of oneself through contact with other people."

The Lucent Books Travel Guide series enlivens history by introducing a new and innovative style and format. Each volume in the series presents the history of a preeminent historical travel destination written in the casual style and format of a travel guide. Whether providing a tour of fifth-century B.C. Athens, Renaissance Florence, or Shakespeare's London, each book describes a city or area at its cultural peak and orients readers to only those places and activities that are known to have existed at that time.

A high level of authenticity is achieved in the Travel Guide series. Each book is written in the present tense and addresses the reader as a prospective foreign traveler. The sense of authenticity is further achieved, whenever possible, by the inclusion of descriptive quotations by contemporary writers who knew the place; information on fascinating historical sites; and travel tips meant to explain unusual cultural idiosyncrasies that give depth and texture to all great cultural centers. Even shopping details, such as where to buy an ermine-trimmed gown or a much-needed house slave, are included to inform readers of what items were sought after throughout history.

Looked at collectively, this series presents an appealing presentation of many of the cultural and social highlights of Western civilization. The collection also provides a framework for discussion about the larger historical currents that dominated not only each travel destination but countries and entire continents as well. Each book is customized by the author to bring to the fore the most important and most interesting characteristics that define each title. High standards of scholarship are assured in the series by the generous peppering of relevant quotes and extensive bibliographies. These tools provide readers a scholastic standard for their own research as well as a guide to direct them to other books, periodicals, and websites that will provide them greater breadth and detail.

INTRODUCTION

Heart of the Midwest

The year is 1929, and America is caught up in the Roaring Twenties, a decade of prosperity and modernization that is unparalleled in the country's history. Businesses are expanding. The stock market is soaring. Most Americans have jobs and go home at night to houses equipped with electric lights, telephones, flush toilets, and built-in bathtubs. Family values are important,

Magnificent skyscrapers tower above Michigan Avenue, a Chicago thoroughfare that constantly bustles with activity.

Tribute

Poet Carl Sandburg was virtually unknown to the literary world when, in 1914, a group of his poems appeared in the nationally circulated Poetry *magazine. His best known, "Chicago" is a tribute to the extraordinary metropolis.*

Hog Butcher for the World,
Tool Maker, Stacker of Wheat,
Player with Railroads and the Nation's Freight Handler;
Stormy, husky, brawling,
City of the Big Shoulders. . . .
Come and show me another city with lifted head singing so proud to be alive and coarse and strong and cunning. . . .
Fierce as a dog with tongue lapping for action, cunning as a savage pitted against the wilderness,
Bareheaded,
Shoveling,
Wrecking,
Planning,
Building, breaking, rebuilding. . . .
Laughing even as an ignorant fighter laughs who has never lost a battle,
Bragging and laughing that under his wrist is the pulse, and under his ribs the heart of the people,
Laughing!
Laughing the stormy, husky, brawling laughter of Youth, half-naked, sweating, proud to be Hog Butcher, Tool Maker, Stacker of Wheat, Player with Railroads and Freight Handler to the Nation.

but people have time for fun and frivolity as well.

Chicago, Illinois, is flourishing along with the rest of America, but it is making newspaper headlines not for prosperity, but for crime and corruption. Prohibition has made alcohol illegal in the United States and has given gangsters like Al Capone and George "Bugs" Moran the opportunity to grow rich as they run illegal breweries, smuggle in liquor from Canada and the Caribbean islands, and finance bootleg (illegal) operations. Their's and other lesser gangs continually jockey for power and try to eliminate each other. Corrupt Chicago politicians and law officials allow crime to flourish almost uninterrupted. Mayor William "Big Bill" Thompson, perhaps one of the most dishonest, shrugs off the lawlessness. "Sure we have crime here," he admits. "We always will have crime. Chicago is just like any other big city."[1]

Americans who are looking for a place to visit might ask why they should come to this controversial city in the heart of the Midwest. The answer is simple. Despite its decadent aspects, Chicago is an exciting place—a metropolitan center—that is prosperous, growing, and full of wholesome as well as sophisticated fun. New hotels, restaurants, department stores, and entertainment facilities are being built all the time. Visitors can go to a baseball game or see some of the finest art and architecture in the world. They can stroll along Lake Michigan or shop for dinnerware and diamonds on State Street. And those who want thrills can drive past Capone's home or seek out the grave of one-time city boss James "Big Jim" Colosimo in Oak Wood Cemetery.

This travel guide is written for everyone who wants to become acquainted with Chicago. Its chapters highlight the city's past and explain how it has grown to greatness. They provide information on how visitors can enjoy an urban vacation safely and securely. They detail the best places to sleep, shop, and play, and focus on some of the city's most famous and infamous citizens. They also explain why 3 million people call Chicago home, and why thousands of visitors come through its gateways each year to see and sample all the treasures it has to offer. As journalist and editor Henry Justin Smith notes, "The city has been studied, loved, hated, praised and denounced. . . . Only in the most indifferent has it failed to awaken an ardent curiosity."[2]

CHAPTER ONE

A Brief History of Chicago

Visitors to Chicago in 1929 will find no hint of the city's origins as they explore its bustling business districts and crowded neighborhoods. French explorers who passed through the region in 1673 saw only low, swampy ground populated by Native Americans who called the land "Checagou" after a kind of wild onion that grew there. In 1803, the U.S. Army built Fort Dearborn where Lake Michigan merged with the Chicago River, but the region remained a desolate spot

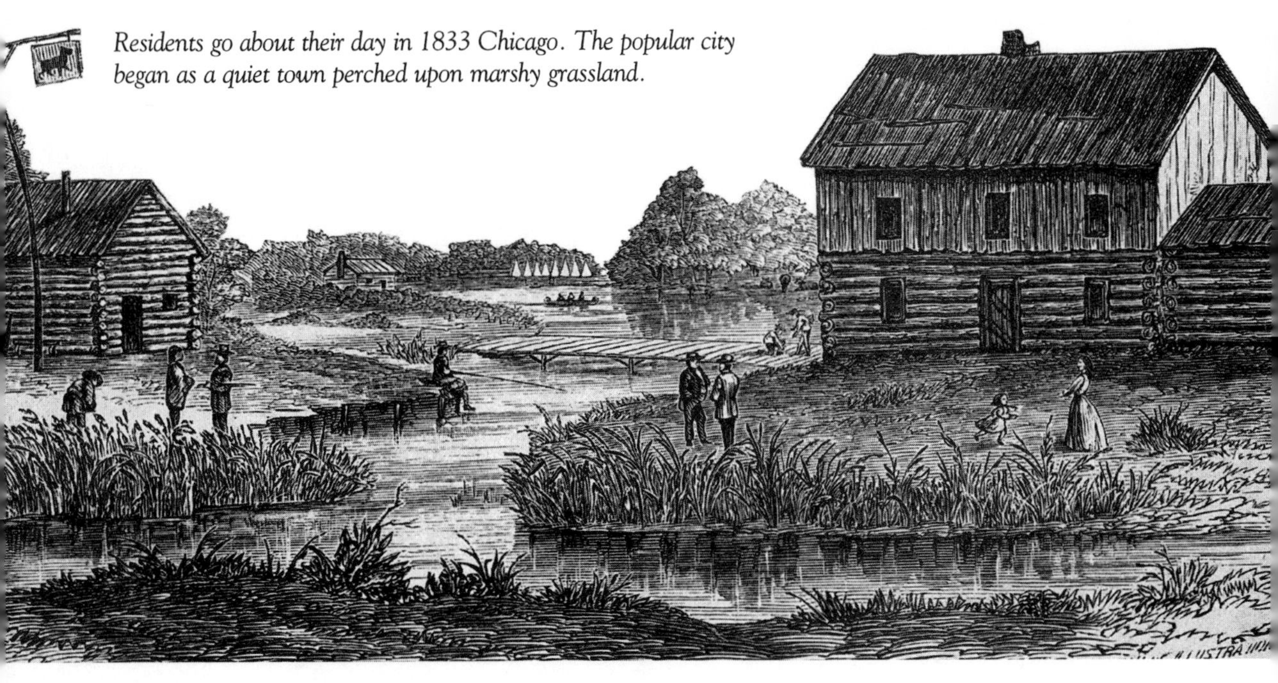

Residents go about their day in 1833 Chicago. The popular city began as a quiet town perched upon marshy grassland.

on the frontier until hostile Indians were forced to move to reservations in Kansas in the mid-1830s.

City of Enterprise

In 1833, Chicago's population stood at about 150 people, and the town was little more than a scattering of shanties, unpainted buildings, and saloons. Living was rough, and unscrupulous merchants and land speculators often exploited those newcomers who settled there. Despite the drawbacks, by 1837, the population of Chicago was over four thousand and included lawyers, doctors, ministers, and teachers. That year, the community was incorporated as a city.

The completion of a canal linking Lake Michigan to the Mississippi River and the coming of the railroads in 1848 spurred more growth. By 1856, Chicago was the hub of ten main railroad lines. The town became an important port and trading center for raw materials from the west and finished goods from the east. The slaughtering and packing industry, which also began in 1848, expanded enormously as millions of cattle, hogs, and sheep were shipped by rail to Chicago for processing.

Enterprising entrepreneurs soon recognized Chicago's potential for wealth and greatness. Cyrus McCormick came to Chicago in 1845 with only $60 in his pocket and made his fortune manufacturing the mechanical reaper, his invention for cutting grain. George Pullman arrived in Chicago in 1855, became wealthy designing and assembling the first railway sleeping cars to be used in long-distance travel, and also built the model town of Pullman for his thousands of employees.

Potter Palmer, a New Yorker who arrived in Chicago in 1852, made his first fortune in a dry goods store that catered expressly to wealthy women. He then expanded his fortune to $8 million by pur-

In 1868 Marshall Field founded his department store, a first-class retailer that is still popular today.

chasing a mile of frontage property on undeveloped State Street and persuading Chicago officials to make it the city's main commercial district. One of Palmer's employees, Marshall Field, bought out Palmer's Dry Goods in 1868, turned it into the renowned Marshall Field and Company department store, and continued Palmer's tradition of providing Chicago shoppers first-class elegance. When he died in 1906, Field left a fortune totaling $120 million.

Wartime Chicago

Men like McCormick, Palmer, and Field were just a few to make money in Chicago. With the coming of the Civil War, the city's railroads and slaughter and meatpacking businesses played a large part in providing tons of meat and grain to the Union Army. Lumber from Wisconsin was also shipped in and out of the city, making it the world's lumber capital. Support services such as banks, wagon and shipbuilding firms, flour and grist (grain) mills, and breweries and distilleries multiplied. So did new department stores, bookstores, jewelry establishments, and furniture houses.

With so many opportunities for work, by 1870 over a quarter of a million people lived in Chicago. British author and member of Parliament Thomas Hughes visited the city and described his impressions in a letter written in September 1870: "This place is the wonder of the Wonderful West. . . . It is one of the handsomest cities I ever saw, with 300,000 inhabitants and progressing [growing] at a rate of 1,500 a week."[3]

About half of the newcomers were foreign born. Germans, Irish, eastern Europeans, and Scandinavians formed the largest groups. Most of these people were poor and lived on the brink of destitution while working hard and hoping for a better life. Some remained trapped in their poverty, but many successfully moved up to a middle-class lifestyle.

Not surprisingly, some of the new arrivals were opportunists, out to make their fortunes quickly. Some were speculators who became involved in a multitude of shady and illegal designs. Some were drifters, vagabonds, and fugitives from the law. Many of these settled in

Mudtown

"Mudtown" was a popular nickname for Chicago in the 1830s. Its mud was known for its depth, stickiness, color, and bad smell. When it rained, unpaved streets became quagmires, and stories were told of street signs that proclaimed "No Bottom Here" and "Short Way to China." An often-repeated tale was of a man sunk so deep in street mud that only his head and shoulders were visible. Asked if he needed help, he answered, "H—, no. I got a horse under me."

Raising Chicago

By the late 1830s, plank streets had been laid in downtown Chicago, but no one paid attention to disposal of sewage and garbage. The city was below lake level, so gravity couldn't take care of drainage and back ups were common. Then a city engineer suggested that the only thing to do was to jack up the buildings and put twelve feet of hard-pack graded earth under them. The streets could be raised as well.

City fathers were so desperate that the plan was put in effect. Beginning in 1855, every structure in town was raised. The job took five years and covered over a thousand acres of construction. Reportedly, many drunken individuals fell to their deaths while staggering and stumbling between the lifted and unlifted sections of streets.

neighborhoods that became notorious for crime. Clark Street from Randolph to Monroe was known as Gambler's Row. Randolph Street between Clark and State Streets was nicknamed "Hairtrigger Block" because gunfights were so common. The Sands region north of the Chicago River was so dangerous that a man could be killed in his bed for his clothes.

By the 1870s, there were so many vice districts in Chicago that a directory was published to enable visitors to identify and avoid them. One visitor dubbed Chicago "the wickedest city in the country."[4] Nevertheless, the town continued to grow and flourish until 1871. At that time, it suffered a tragedy of such epic proportions that its history would be marked by the event forever.

Tragedy and Triumph

On the night of October 8, 1871—a warm, windy Sunday evening—fire broke out in or near the Patrick O'Leary barn on Chicago's West Side. Denis Sullivan, a neighbor of the O'Learys, raised the alarm about 9:00 P.M. after he smelled smoke and noticed flames flickering in the darkness.

Fires were fairly common in Chicago. Barns were full of hay and straw. Homes, fences, and outbuildings were made of wood, which easily burned at the slightest spark. So despite the promptness of Sullivan's call, the flames soon turned into a roaring blaze that spread out of control. Fanned by a strong southwest wind, the fire jumped the river's southern and central branches, and swept through slums and business districts where warehouses, sidewalks, and storefronts were also made of wood. Factories, theaters, businesses, and wealthy neighborhoods burned to the ground. Rich and poor residents alike fled from their homes and took shelter along the lakeshore, on the prairie outside the city, and even in open graves in an abandoned cemetery south of Lincoln Park.

Two days later, as the fire burned itself out, one third of Chicago lay in ruins. Three and a half square miles had been burned, and 17,450 buildings were lost. One thousand people were left homeless, and between 250 and 500 had perished. Monetary losses were estimated to be at least $200 million.

The tragedy brought out the best in Chicagoans, however. As homes and businesses were rebuilt, city officials made sure that fire laws and building regulations were stricter. Businessmen modernized their facilities. Architects designed taller and sturdier structures. Public transportation systems developed, and those who could afford to ride a train or streetcar to work resettled in the burgeoning suburbs. Streets were paved. Streetlights were installed. All the growth and modernization helped make Chicago one of the most progressive cities in the world. The *Chicago Tribune* commented in 1873:

> It is a common remark that Chicago was set forward ten years by the fire. The mingled town and village aspects are gone. . . . The tendency is to the metropolitan in everything, buildings and their uses, stores and their occupants. And village notions are passing away with them. . . . No one expects to know . . . half the audience at the church or theater, and as for knowing one's neighbors, that has become a lost art.[5]

World-Class City

Chicago had always been a popular destination of immigrants, but between 1880 and 1920 3.5 million newcomers arrived from Russia, Poland, Italy, and other parts of eastern Europe. During World War I (1914–1918), southern blacks also began migrating north in great numbers, seeking economic opportunities. Again, most found life in the city to be more difficult than they had expected, but with the help of humanitarian reformers like Jane Addams and Ellen Gates Starr, conditions they endured gradually improved.

A young newspaper vendor hawks the famous headline about the devastating Chicago fire of 1871.

By 1890, Chicago was the second largest city in the United States, surpassed only by New York. In 1893, to draw attention to the city's accomplishments, officials successfully lobbied to have the World's Columbian Exposition, a world's fair, held in their town. The event observed the four hundredth anniversary of Christopher Columbus's arrival in America. The fair's chief architect was Daniel H. Burnham, whose grand design with its monumental buildings and precise layout had enormous influence on town-planning in later decades. Hundreds of thousands of visitors came to the exposition, marveling at the fair's pools, fountains, and gleaming white buildings.

Genesis of Organized Crime

Organized crime came to Chicago around the beginning of the twentieth century. At its head was James "Big Jim" Colosimo, an Italian American who got his start in "the Levee," another notorious vice district in the city. Colosimo specialized in managing prostitution rings and had ties to politics as well. Two of his best friends were corrupt Chicago aldermen (representatives) Michael "Hinky Dink" McKenna and "Bathhouse" John Coughlin, who ensured that Colosimo's illegal establishments could operate in exchange for bribes and payoffs. Mayor William "Big Bill" Thompson, elected in 1917, was another politician who allowed Colosimo's enterprises to prosper.

Around 1908, Colosimo's illegal business activities became so complex and time consuming that he decided he needed an assistant. He chose a New Yorker named John Torrio to be his new second in command. Over the next ten years, Torrio capably coped with politicians, police, and rival gangs such as the Genna brothers, the O'Donnells, and Dion O'Banion's North Side gang. When Prohibition made liquor illegal in 1920, he recognized that money could be made producing and selling the banned substance. After an unknown gunman killed Colosimo that same year, Torrio became the city's top bootlegger as well as a major power in Chicago's underworld.

For his own second in command, Torrio brought in a tough young New Yorker named Al Capone. Capone, an Italian American with immigrant parents, was just twenty-one years old when he arrived in Chicago in 1920, but he quickly proved to be cunning, ambitious, and ruthless. Capone never hesitated to use intimidation, bribery, and force to achieve his ends, although today he tries to hide his viciousness behind a winning smile and ingratiating ways. He also portrays himself as a family man and a misunderstood businessman when reporters interview him. "I've been spending the best years of my life as a public benefactor," he said recently. "I've given people the light pleasures, shown them a good time. And all I get is abuse."[6] Despite his attempts, he cannot conceal the fact that he methodically continues to do away with his opponents, take over legitimate businesses, and bring police and politicians under his influence.

White City

Chicago's World's Columbian Exposition was held between May and October 1893, and gave almost 30 million visitors a chance to see that the city had recovered from the Great Fire of 1871 and had become a cosmopolitan center.

The exposition was enormous, covering over six hundred acres. Its imposing buildings, built in classical style and painted white, earned it the name "White City." Its steam plant generated three times more electricity than that used by the city itself. The Midway Plaisance, an open space dedicated to entertainment, allowed visitors to watch a balloon ascension, visit an Austrian village, view the Eiffel Tower in miniature, or take a ride in the first Ferris wheel in the world. The latter stood 250 feet tall and featured 36 cars that could hold up to 60 people each.

The exposition marked many other "firsts" for America as well. Due to the exposure they received, Cracker Jacks, Juicy Fruit gum, diet soda, and hamburgers all became hugely popular with the public and remain so today.

The Manufactures and Liberal Arts Building, which housed the World's Columbian Exposition in 1893, features a soaring 312-foot-high roof.

Al Capone is notorious for his shady business practices and use of force as means to achieve his ends.

Since Capone took over leadership of Chicago's underworld from Torrio in 1925, lawbreaking has reached new heights in the city. Crime has spread to the suburbs, where there are more speakeasies, brothels (houses of prostitution), and gambling dens than ever before. Many Chicagoans are willing to tolerate the lawlessness not only because Prohibition is unpopular, but also because they find that fun is better when it skirts close to danger. The state of affairs is regrettable, but city officials and ordinary people alike quickly point out that visitors need not feel personally threatened as they tour the city and enjoy its many attractions. Public shootouts are rare occurrences, and gangsters, if and when they kill, usually kill each other. Robberies and assaults are common only after dark in bad sections of town.

In fact, 1929 is a fabulous time to come to Chicago, where the shopping, the sightseeing, and the nightlife are incomparable. So for those who love good food, great jazz, and a variety of entertainment, come to one of the most multifaceted and metropolitan places in the Midwest. It will be a unique and unforgettable experience.

CHAPTER TWO

Preparing for a Visit

Chicago, a city of over 3 million people, is located in northeastern Illinois, along the shore of Lake Michigan at the mouth of the Chicago River. The river forms a Y, flowing west from the lake through the downtown area, and then forking into the north and south branches. It divides the city into three geographic zones: north, south, and west.

Chicago's natural landscape is flat, and Lake Michigan, the third largest of the Great Lakes, is a very visible part of the setting. It runs the length of the eastern edge of the city, feeds the Chicago River, and helps moderate the city's Midwestern weather.

When to Go and What to Pack

When planning a trip to Chicago, remember to take weather into account. Residents testify that it can change dramatically from day to day and sometimes even from hour to hour. Summers are often hot and humid, with temperatures in the 80s and 90s. Thunderstorms can arise in the afternoon. Winters are cold and raw with temperatures falling well below 20 degrees. Blizzards sometimes whip the region, and northern Illinois gets an average of thirty inches of snow a year. During the spring and fall, temperature and weather are more moderate and comfortable. Come during these seasons to enjoy all the outdoor sights and entertainment the city has to offer.

When packing for a summer trip to Chicago, light clothing is the rule. Heavier wear is best for winter. During cold, windy weather, heavy coats, warm gloves, and mufflers are recommended. Good walking shoes, however, are a must in any season. Those visitors coming from rural areas and concerned about looking appropriate can pack outfits suitable for church. Those who want to enjoy the lake and city beaches during

good weather should remember to pack swimming suits and perhaps a beach umbrella. If you forget something, however, remember that Chicago has some of the largest department stores in the nation where you can purchase anything you need.

How to Get There

For those who want to travel to Chicago by air, the Chicago Municipal Airport opened in late 1927. Located southwest of town, and bounded by Cicero and South Central Avenues and West 59th and West 63rd Streets, the facility is just a taxi drive from the city.

In this day of automobile traffic, driving to Chicago is feasible. Improved highway systems are making travel faster and easier. Increasing numbers of service stations, restaurants, hotels, and auto camps are available to provide services for travelers en route. It is wise, however, to prepare for unexpected breakdowns and pack water, tire patching materials, and a roll of baling wire for clamping looses hoses and reattaching fenders and exhaust pipes.

Because Chicago is the top railroad center of the nation, the most popular way to journey there is by train. Those who live within several hundred miles of the city may be able to use one of several interurban electric train lines that service the area. For instance, the North Shore Line runs between Milwaukee, Wisconsin, and Chicago, while the South Shore Line operates between South Bend, Indiana, and Chicago. Both make stops along their lines.

The Pennsylvania, Illinois Central, Santa Fe, and Milwaukee Railroads, as well as a host of other rail lines, link Chicago with eastern and western cities as far away as Miami and Seattle. All the comforts of travel can be enjoyed on streamlined expresses such as the 20th Century Limited and Super Chief. At the end of the journey, passengers should also take a moment to admire the vast concourses and ornate exteriors of Chicago's enormous train depots: Union Station's massive lobby, Illinois Central's Victorian façade, Dearborn's twelve-story Romanesque clock tower, and Chicago and Northwestern's six huge granite columns that rise more than sixty feet above street level. "We find ourselves in the gigantic vestibule of a large city," one awed traveler observes as he walks through one of these stations. "The space encloses thousands of people in any single minute and then disperses them in all directions in the next."[7]

Getting Around

Because Chicago is so large, walking is not a practical way of seeing all the sights. Many restaurants, stores, and nightclubs are within walking distance of hotels in the downtown section, however. Driving one's car in the city is possible, but traffic can be extremely congested.

As alternatives, a wide variety of public transportation options are available. Yellow and Checker taxicabs are everywhere and are easy to flag down. Streetcars and city buses are both efficient and inexpensive. The well-known "L" (elevated) trains run from the Loop (downtown Chicago) to the suburbs as well. They are required riding for any visitor wanting to experience all Chicago has to

Flowing Backward

In 1900, the Chicago River became famous as "the river that flows backward" after Chicago engineers reversed the current to stop the city's sewage from polluting Lake Michigan, Chicago's water supply. The feat was carried out by deepening the bed of the Chicago Sanitary and Ship Canal, which paralleled and then ran into the south branch of the river, and then installing powerful pumps to help move the water along. Not surprisingly, the system was not perfect, but it emphasized the fact that Chicagoans were capable of doing big things in a big way.

Overnighters

When planning to spend the night on a train, passengers should be aware that sleeping conditions are comfortable, but not luxurious. Older model Pullman coaches, designed in 1907, commonly include a lounge with toilet facilities, one men's and one women's dressing room, and twelve sleeping sections consisting of upper and lower berths with hallway curtains. Berths are large enough to hold one adult. Electricity is supplied from generators attached to the car's axles. A newer model car, introduced in 1927, includes as many as fourteen sleeping compartments with doors for greater privacy. Each compartment is equipped with its own bed, toilet, and folding washstand.

In all cases, however, space is limited, and travelers will be wise to carry only the essentials on board.

offer. Street guides and bus and elevated timetables are widely available.

City Layout

Chicago can be generally divided into three sections, all defined by the Chicago River. Bearing that in mind, with a brief overview and a good map, visitors can be confident that they will not miss anything they want to see while in town.

North Side. Chicago's North Side—located north of the Chicago River—is characterized by business and residential neighborhoods. Uptown, a leading retail and entertainment district for North Side Chicagoans lies between Lawrence and Montrose Avenues. For those who want good shopping and bright lights outside the Loop district, this is an option. Lincoln Park, a one-thousand-acre park east of Uptown, is the city's largest green space. The Astor Street and Lake Shore Drive districts, tree-lined neighborhoods of Chicago's well-to-do residents, also lie on the North Side.

South Side. Chicago's South Side—located south of the river—includes the Loop, a one-half-square-mile district centered along South State Street. The Loop is the heart of Chicago and has some of the finest hotels, restaurants, department stores, and nightspots the city has to offer. The Loop is also home to city hall and Chicago's banking and financial center.

South of the Loop, Chinatown is a small but colorful neighborhood where visitors can get a taste of Asian culture and cuisine. Hyde Park and the University of Chicago with its Gothic spires are just a short ten-mile drive south of the Loop.

The Union Stock Yards lie west of Hyde Park. Here, millions of cattle, sheep, and pigs are processed (slaughtered) each year, evidence that Chicago is the meatpacking capital of the United States.

Packingtown, home to many of the city's newest immigrants, lies southwest of the yards.

West Side. The West Side, lying west of the north and south branches of the Chicago River, is home to a large proportion of Chicago's ethnic population. Halsted Street is just one neighborhood that bustles with street vendors, bargain hunters, small markets, and businesses.

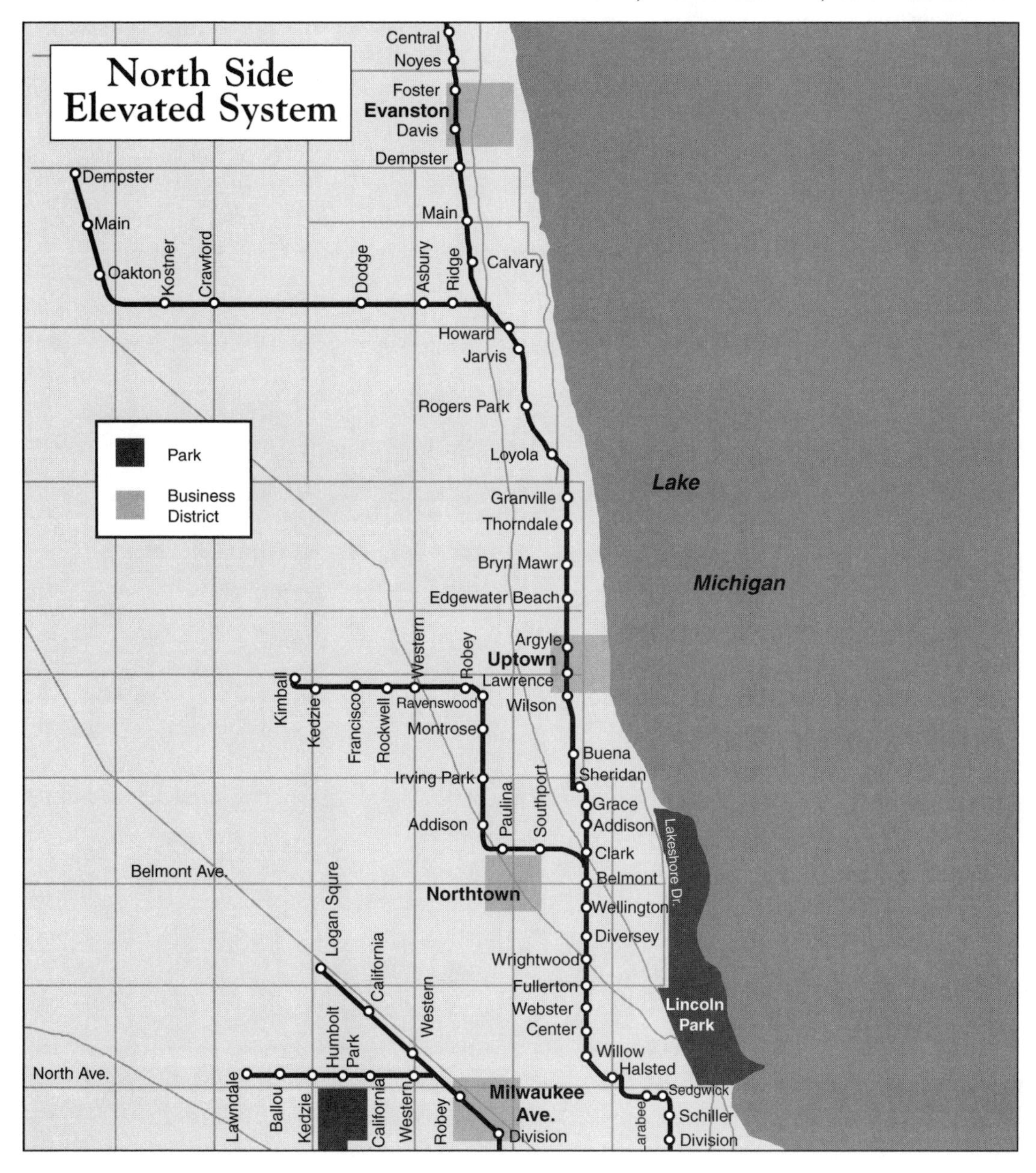

Pullman Porters

Every traveler is familiar with Pullman porters who act as attendants on America's passenger trains. But most are unaware that porters were the inspiration of Chicago industrialist George Pullman, who "equipped" his sleeping cars with highly trained black men when the cars were leased by a railroad. Originally, the cars were staffed with freed slaves, whom Pullman felt were skilled in service and willing to work for low wages.

Today, the Pullman Rail Car Company is the largest employer of blacks in the country. The position is highly respected in the black community because it offers a steady income, an opportunity to travel across America, and a life largely free of heavy physical labor. The greatest number of Pullman porters live on Chicago's South Side.

Passenger-train travelers will surely be satisfied with shoe shines and other services provided by Pullman porters.

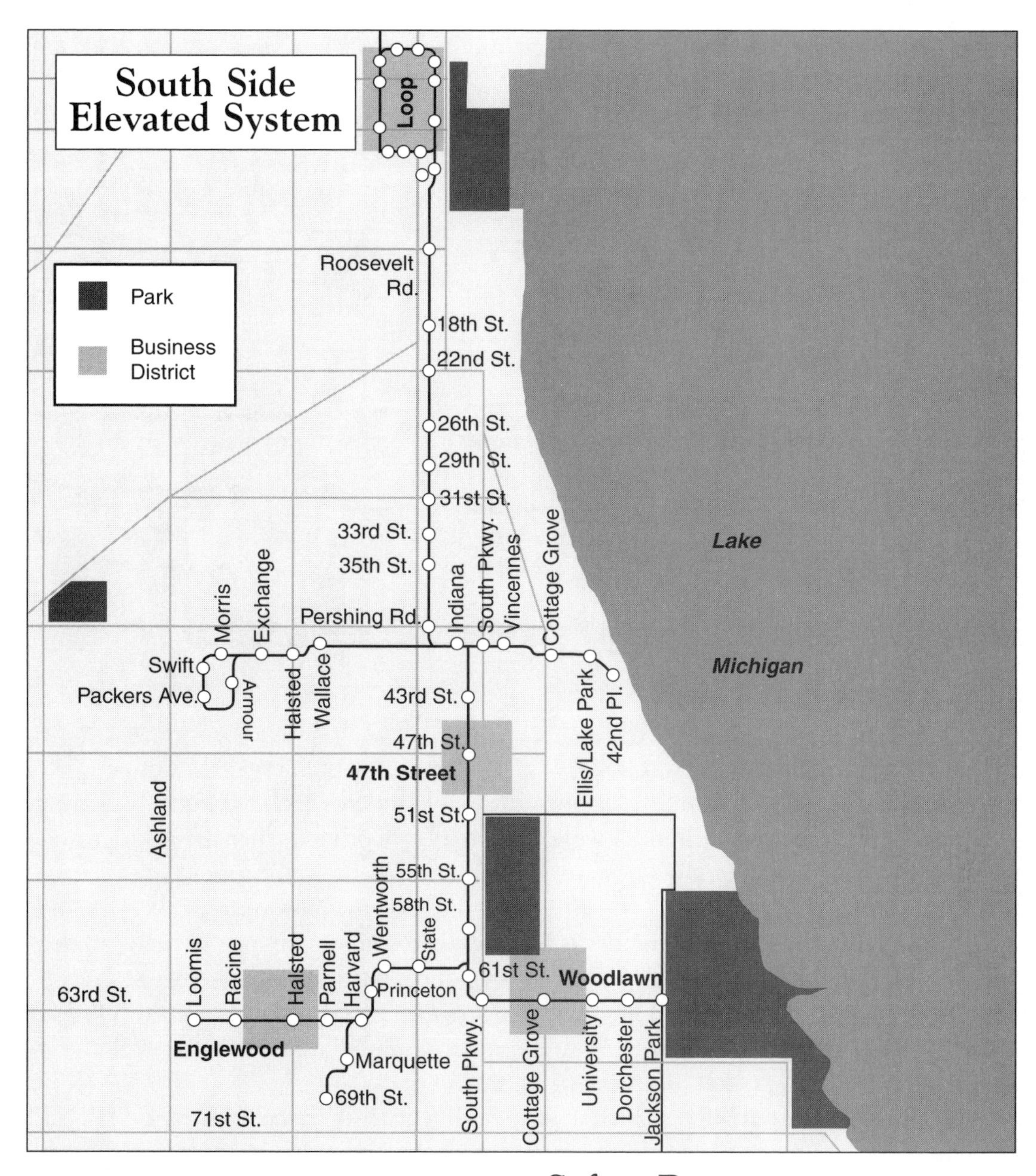

Chicago has many West Side suburbs, but the most notorious is Cicero, a neighborhood of hard-working immigrants that has been taken over by Al Capone and his henchmen.

Safety Precautions

Despite Chicago's reputation for wild times and lawlessness, most of its residents are ordinary, law-abiding citizens. The chance of being gunned

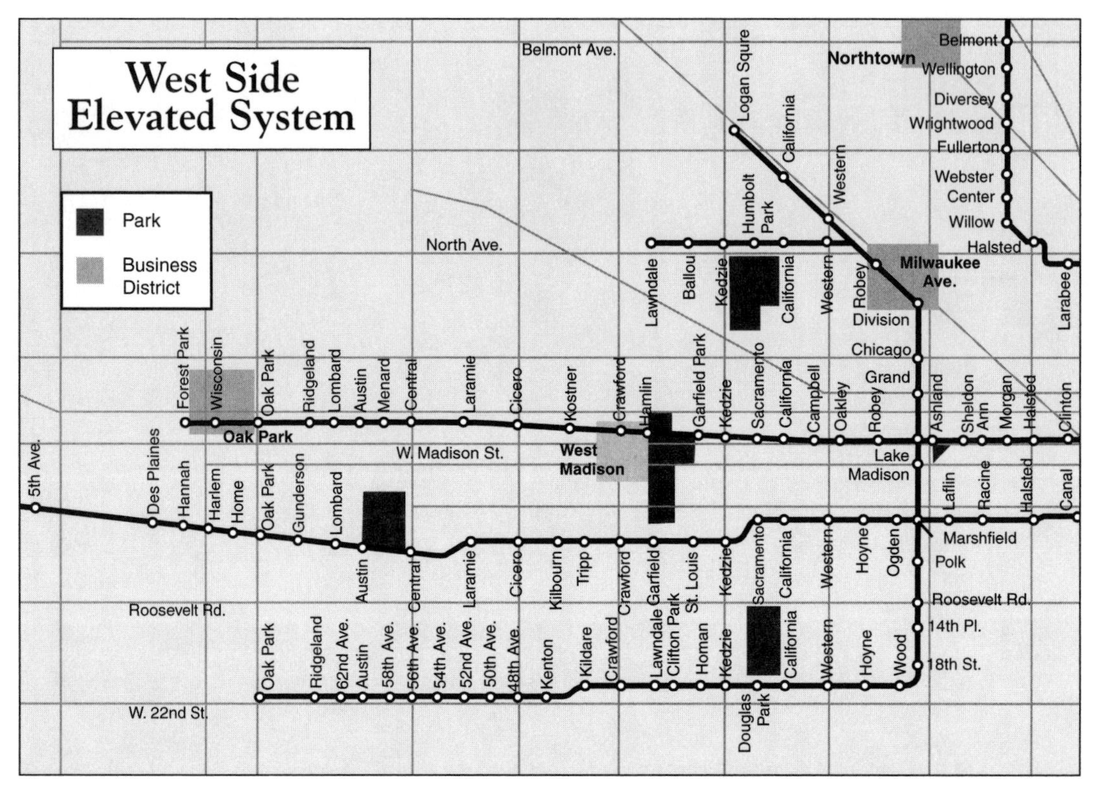

down on the street is very low. Unwary visitors, however, may become victims of pickpockets, purse snatchers, jewelry thieves, and con artists if they are not careful.

To ward off unfortunate incidents, take precautions that are standard in any large city. Ladies, hold purses and satchels securely with both hands. Men, keep wallets in a front coat pocket. Beware of strangers who jostle or engage in loud arguments—they could be distracting your attention while another person grabs your valuables. Look alert and purposeful as you walk, and when boarding a streetcar or train, have your fare ready. Never leave parcels unattended.

Especially at night, stay out of questionable suburbs such as Cicero and away from neighborhoods such as Packingtown, behind the Union Stock Yards. Those who choose to patronize speakeasies and nightclubs take a chance of being raided by police, but since many of these law officers are bribed to overlook Prohibition violations, the risk of arrest is relatively small.

If you should be injured or fall ill, hotel management or any police officer can call an ambulance or direct you to a doctor or one of Chicago's fine hospital facilities. Mercy Hospital, the first hospital to be established in the city, is located on 26th Street and Calumet Avenue,

Union Station

Union Station, which occupies ten city blocks between Adams and Jackson Streets, opened in May 1925 and was declared, "America's latest triumph in railroading" by Mayor William "Decent" Dever. It is one of the largest train stations to be built in the twentieth century and easily accommodates the one hundred through it daily.

At the entrance of the station is the main concourse, where passengers walk beneath a ninety-foot-high, skylighted ceiling on their way to the trains. A Travelers' Aid Society booth is nearby to give assistance to stranded visitors or advice to those who are unfamiliar with the city. The station's huge waiting room with its pink Tennessee marble floors and massive wooden benches is a haven for those with long layovers. Concessions such as shoe shine and newspaper stands cater to businessmen. Those who are hungry will find restaurants and snack shops nearby.

The expansive Union Station receives thousands of travelers and one hundred trains every day.

and is considered one of the nation's greatest medical institutions. Cook County Hospital is located on Harrison Street and is a two-thousand-bed facility distinguished by its medical advancements. Provident Hospital on 36th Street on the South Side is another fine facility that is proud to be the first black hospital in the United States.

Accommodations

Chicago has dozens of hotels, from the Alcazar on Washington Boulevard to the Windemere on East 56th Street. Most facilities that are designed to please the discriminating traveler are located in the Loop, Uptown, and along the beach. They offer spacious rooms, stately lobbies, and a wide range of services including barbershops, bellhops, top-notch restaurants, and prime evening entertainment.

Finding food in Chicago is even easier than finding a hotel. Everything from sandwiches to pheasant under glass is available. Whether it's a hot dog at the beach, a soda at a department store lunch counter, or a plate of chow mein in Chinatown, visitors can find something good to eat wherever they go.

Hotel Atlantic, Clark Street near Jackson Boulevard. For those looking for

A Ride on the "L"

Attractive young women be warned! "L" guards have a reputation for gallantry, and a ride in their cars can have an unexpected outcome. An article entitled "Admit Flirting on the L" in the May 25, 1902, edition of the Chicago Daily Tribune *explains the risks, which may or may not have lessened over time.*

"The girls are pretty, so why shouldn't we flirt?" asked a guard on the Metropolitan Elevated yesterday.

And he was not the only guard who was willing to admit that his conception of his duties included flirting with girl passengers.

"I won my wife on this same car," declared a guard on the South Side Elevated. "She was employed in a glue factory over near the river, and rode downtown on the 6:38 every morning. For several weeks I opened the gate for her, and soon came to be disappointed when occasionally she missed my train. One morning I told her that if she ever missed connections again I'd jump into the lake. She laughed at me and called me a 'jollier' [joker]. I pleaded not guilty, but noticed that after that she never missed my train. Well, there isn't much to the story. Last summer Justice Wallace performed the ceremony."

a modest hotel, the 450-room Atlantic offers comfort and economy. Rooms start at $1.50 per night.

LaSalle Hotel, North LaSalle at Madison Street. The LaSalle prides itself on catering to the tastes of ladies as well as gentlemen. Its roof gardens are both lovely and sophisticated. Some of Chicago's most famous society matrons including Bertha Palmer, wife of Potter Palmer, dine regularly at the LaSalle's elegant Blue Fountain Room restaurant.

Drake Hotel, North Michigan Avenue and Lake Shore Drive. With views of Lake Michigan, this impressive facility, built in 1920, offers every luxury from velvet seats in its elevators to a basket of fresh fruit in each room. Its lobby, public rooms, guest rooms, and corridors are spacious and beautifully appointed. The Drake is expensive, but worth every penny if you want to experience opulence.

Morrison Hotel, West Madison and Clark Streets. This forty-six-story hotel, reportedly the world's tallest, is one of the premier places to stay in Chicago. Guests can enjoy its elegant lobby with marble front desk, dine at its popular Boston Oyster House, and experience its Terrace Garden dinner theater.

Palmer House, South State at Monroe Street. This posh hotel was originally a gift from millionaire Potter Palmer to his wife. It features oversized rooms, luxurious décor, and delicious meals. One of its many elegancies includes a barbershop floor tiled with silver dollars. Note that after the Great Fire of 1871, the Palmer House was rebuilt with safety in mind and now advertises itself as the "only thoroughly fireproof hotel in the United States."[8]

The landmark Sherman House Hotel offers luxurious rooms and a staff dedicated to pampering their guests.

Sherman House Hotel, North Clark at Randolph Street. Reportedly the largest hotel west of New York City, the Sherman has sixteen hundred guest rooms and a banquet hall that seats twenty-five hundred. Mayor William "Big Bill" Thompson held his victory celebration in its magnificent Louis XIV Ballroom in 1927. Its College Inn Restaurant features fine food and some of the best jazz in the city.

As a point of interest, Capone chose the Sherman as the locale for a much publicized gangster conference held on October 20, 1926. Attendees included Capone, George "Bugs" Moran, William "Klondike" and Myles O'Donnell, and several others. During the meeting, the gunmen agreed to a limited peace treaty that brought calm to Chicago's gangland for a time.

Berghoff Restaurant, 17 West Adams Street. German-born Herman Joseph Berghoff, who comes from the city of Dortmund, opened the Berghoff Café in 1898 to showcase his notable Dortmunder-style beer. Berghoff's beer sold for a nickel and sandwiches were free. Today, the restaurant specializes in near beer (nonalcoholic beer) and Bergo Soda Pop, and has expanded to a full-service restaurant. Enjoy its tasty food and tasteful interior.

Schulien's, 2100 West Irving Park Road. An old-world German restaurant and bar that offers traditional German entrees, Schulien's in north Chicago is one of Capone's hangouts. Entertainment in the restaurant is unique. For a donation, magician Harry Blackstone Sr. will perform a ten-minute show at your table after your meal.

Thompson's Cafeterias, the Loop, Uptown, and other districts. Thompson's Cafeterias are a good bet when it comes to grabbing a bite to eat. With over twenty locales in the Loop alone, there is a good chance that one will be nearby when hunger strikes. Thompson's caters to everyone from factory workers to department store shoppers and offers nutritious, inexpensive meals. Because most Thompson's are open late (some are open twenty-four hours a day), they are attractive to night owls, artists, and after-theater crowds.

Chicago Neighborhoods

Anyone who comes to Chicago for a visit will quickly discover that the city is too big to see in its entirety. Everything seems oversized—the lake, the buildings, the streets, and the crowds. One way to get a good overview in a short period of time is to visit various neighborhoods. Spending a few hours in them will give a glimpse of the variety of people, places, sights, and sounds that make up the city.

Gold Coast

This North Side district, made fashionable by social-climbing industrialists and other well-to-do residents, includes the neighborhood around Astor Street and Lake Shore Drive. Stroll or drive along the shady avenues where you'll see grand mansions and luxury apartments. The following mansions are just a few of the residences in the vicinity. Take time to explore; all are impressive.

Palmer Castle, 1350 North Lake Shore Drive, between Banks and Schiller Streets. In the 1880s, retail and real estate mogul Potter Palmer had this graystone imitation Rhenish castle built on

A style of architecture rare anywhere in America is featured in Chicago's Palmer Castle, a must-see for tourists.

what was a stretch of dune and marsh. At the time, it was the most imposing private home in Chicago, and is still an awe-inspiring structure with its turrets, towers, and decorative stonework. To ensure privacy, the home has no outdoor locks or doorknobs, and visitors are allowed to enter by appointment only.

Patterson-McCormick Mansion, 1500 Astor Street. This mansion, one of the largest houses on the street, was commissioned by *Chicago Tribune* owner Joseph Medill in 1891 as a wedding gift for his daughter Cissy and her husband Robert Patterson. Cyrus McCormick bought the mansion in 1927. The magnificent brick and terra cotta residence is a fine example of Renaissance revival style.

Archbishop's Residence, 1555 North State Street. This stately Queen Anne-style mansion was built in 1880 to house the archbishop of the Roman Catholic Church. Notice its steeply pitched roof and nineteen chimneys.

Charnley House, 1365 North Astor Street. This orange Roman brick and limestone residence is not a traditional-looking home. It is the work of two renowned American architects, Louis Henri Sullivan and Frank Lloyd Wright, designed in 1892 for lumberman James Charnley. The severe block of the ground floor, coupled with the jutting second-story balcony and clean-cut rectangular windows, contributes to its unique look.

Black Chicago

Chicago's large black population lives south of the Loop in a region bounded by State Street, Cottage Grove Avenue, and 22nd and 55th Streets. The district is virtually a city within a city. Associated with such notables as trumpet player Louis Armstrong and organizer of the National Association for the Advancement of Colored People Ida B. Wells, it offers commercial and cultural opportunities that blacks are denied in other parts of Chicago.

Refer to chapter eight for more information about clubs, theaters, and jazz hotspots in black Chicago including the Savoy Ballroom, Regal Theater, Sunset Café, and Plantation Café. Other notable locales in the neighborhood include the following:

Chicago Defender Building, 3435 South Indiana Avenue. Formerly a Jewish synagogue, the building is now home to the *Chicago Defender*, a newspaper nationally renowned for its outspoken editorial policies on behalf of civil rights. The "Great Black Migration" of southern blacks beginning in 1915 was largely due to the *Chicago Defender*'s insistence that greater opportunities for blacks existed in the northern United States.

Victory Monument, 35th Street and South Park Boulevard. This monument, made up of a circular gray granite shaft inset with three life-sized bronze figures, honors the all-black 8th Illinois Regiment that served in World War I.

Louis Armstrong's Home, 421 East 44th Street. The residence of this jazz great is a comfortable house, large enough to house Armstrong, his wife Lil Hardin, her mother, and Armstrong's adopted son Clarence. The living room with its baby grand piano has been the frequent gathering spot of many musicians such as jazz pianist Jelly Roll Morton and bandleader Joe "King" Oliver who enjoy playing music late into the night.

Schorling's Park, 39th Street between Princeton and Shields Avenues. This small park with its tiny grandstand served as the home of the Chicago White Sox until June 1910 when the club moved to Comiskey Park. The grounds were then leased to John Schorling, a white South Side businessman. The park now serves as the home of one of black baseball's oldest and most powerful teams, the Chicago American Giants, owned and managed by Hall of Fame pitcher Rube Foster. Foster also founded the Negro National League, which included the Chicago (Illinois) Giants, the Chicago American Giants, the Dayton (Ohio) Marcos, the Detroit (Michigan) Stars, the Indianapolis (Indiana) ABCs, the Kansas City (Missouri) Monarchs, the St. Louis (Missouri) Giants, and a traveling Cuban team called the Stars. During the 1920s, the Chicago American Giants won two Negro World Series championships and six league championships.

Willie Foster, pitcher for the Chicago American Giants, follows through on a powerful throw to home plate. Visitors can join local fans at exciting baseball games all summer.

Hyde Park

Established in 1850, Hyde Park is more than Chicago's first South Side suburb. It is a residential area and home to some of Chicago's oldest families such as meatpacker Gustavus F. Swift and Sears, Roebuck executive Julius Rosenwald. It was the site of the World's Columbian Exposition of 1893, and today is the location of the University of Chicago with its stately buildings and reputation for scholarship. At the end of the Midway Plaisance, a broad stretch of green along the edge of the campus, sits the Fountain of Time, a haunting sculpture created in 1922 by Lorado Taft. The fountain depicts the figure of Time observing humanity as it passes by.

Pullman

On the far South Side of Chicago lies the model industrial town of Pullman, built between 1880 and 1884 at the order of George Pullman, founder of the Pullman Palace Car Company. Dissatisfied with working-class living conditions, Pullman purchased four thousand acres of land west of Lake Calumet and built a pleasant, clean, modern community for those who worked for his company.

Pullman community, which received an award in 1896 as the "World's Most Perfect Town," prospered as a self-sufficient model for only fourteen years. Pullman died in 1897, and the Illinois Supreme Court required that the company sell its nonindustrial property. The houses have been privately owned since 1907. The City of Chicago annexed the town along with Hyde Park Township in 1889 and now manages the parks, streets, and school system.

Pullman remains an interesting community to visit. Its centrally located clock tower overlooks one of the most beautiful industrial landscapes in America. The grand, Queen Anne-style Hotel Florence (named for Pullman's daughter) has fifty rooms, a dining room, and the only bar in the community. Its sixteen-foot-wide veranda allows for views of the community's broad shady streets.

Pullman's modest brick homes are well constructed with many modern conveniences. The streets and parks are pleasantly landscaped. The town includes public facilities such as stores and office buildings. A bank, library, theater, post office, and church are close by as well.

Pilsen

Located between Canal and Damen Streets, about three miles south of the Loop, this South Side neighborhood is home to the nation's largest settlement of immigrants, the majority of them Czechoslovakian. In fact, Pilsen derives its name from a Czech town of that name.

Chicago's railroad network is centered in Pilsen, and many large industries relocated here after the Great Fire of 1871. The area has become known as a manufacturing district and a center for national labor movements, although it is primarily a residential district.

Schoenhofen Brewery, 18th Street and Canalport Avenue. The Schoenhofen Brewery was one of the pioneer industries in the Pilsen area, established in 1886 by German American brewer Peter Schoenhofen. By the late nineteenth century, Schoenhofen's was the sixth largest brewery in the United States, brewing 180,000 barrels each year. Today, it is closed due to Prohibition.

The brewery's administration building is a good example of the ornate designs of the late Victorian era, while the powerhouse, constructed in 1902, is in Frank Lloyd Wright's prairie school design. It makes a bold impact with its stark façade and ornamental brickwork.

McCormick Reaper Works, Blue Island and Western Avenues. In 1910, Cyrus McCormick built this factory, one of the largest in the nation, in Pilsen. The McCormick Reaper Works was one of the city's fastest growing and most important industries, and employed thousands of Chicagoans.

McCormick died on May 13, 1884. On August 12, 1902, the McCormick Reaper Works joined with Deering Harvester Company, Plano Harvester Company, Milwaukee Harvester Company, and Warder, Bushnell and Glessner Company, to form International Harvester Company. Cyrus H. McCormick Jr. was named its new president.

St. Procopius Church, 18th and Allport Streets. Built in 1887 by the Benedictine monks of St. Procopius Abbey, the massive St. Procopius Church serves as the "mother church" for Chicago's West Side Czechoslovakians. It has the largest Czech congregation in the United States.

Union Stock Yards

Not everyone will want to visit the enormous Union Stock Yards, whose stone entrance sits at 4100 South Halsted Street. The smells that hang over the

Despite the unfortunate imposition of Prohibition, the Schoenhofen Brewery building can still be appreciated today for its Frank Lloyd Wright façade.

For tourists who can tolerate the odor, the vast cattle pens of the Union Stock Yards are visually striking.

complex are often foul enough to turn the strongest stomach. Nevertheless, the yards are noteworthy because no other city has anything like them. Princes, writers, and intellectuals make them a stop on their tour of Chicago. Thousands of tourists visit them every year.

The yards were established in 1865 in order to centralize the city's multiple stock yards and make the meat packing business more efficient. Today, they are a vast complex of cattle pens, processing and packinghouses, belching smokestacks, and freight yards. Swift and Company, Armour and Company, and other meatpacking companies have their offices on the premises. Over seventy-five thousand Chicagoans—most of them immigrants—are employed there. Most make their homes in Packingtown, an ugly, neglected neighborhood behind the yards that has been the object of reformers' efforts for years.

Little Italy

Visitors will know they have entered Little Italy, centered on Taylor and Halsted Streets, by the scent of bootleg whiskey in the air. At the beginning of Prohibition, a group of lawless Italian American brothers, the Gennas, obtained government authorization to make "in-

Meatpacking Moguls

Philip D. Armour and Gustavus F. Swift, two of Chicago's meatpacking moguls, came to the city in 1875 and made their fortunes processing beef and pork and selling it to buyers in the eastern United States and elsewhere.

Both men established their companies' headquarters in the Union Stock Yards, where they could keep watch over every aspect of their business. Both worked diligently to eliminate waste in their operations and eventually found uses for every part of the animals they processed. Their development of glue, fertilizer, soap, knife handles, and hundreds of other products made from animal products swelled their incomes, and culminated in the jest, "The Chicago packers use every part of the hog but his squeal," as quoted in Lloyd Lewis and Henry Justin Smith's, *Chicago*.

Meatpacking is big business in Chicago. Here employees of Armour and Company make sausage from the less highly prized parts of the pig.

dustrial alcohol," and then set up many of their neighbors as "alky cookers," redistilling bootleg alcohol in their homes in small copper stills. At a time when most residents of Little Italy could barely make $2 a day doing honest work, families who worked for the Gennas were paid $15 a day simply to mind their stills and siphon off the liquor.

The Gennas were murdered in 1924, but bootlegging continues in the neighborhood. Nevertheless, the majority of Italian immigrants are hardworking, law-abiding citizens, putting in long days on the railroads, in the garment industry, or as small businessmen. Visitors will see streets of tenement houses, small homes, and apartments over small shops. Vendors, open markets, and children make the streets lively and colorful. Locally owned grocery stores are good places to buy fruits and vegetables.

The Ferrara Pan Candy Company, 2200 West Taylor Street. Salvatore Ferrara founded Ferrara Company in 1908 as a retail pastry and confection shop, and the present factory was constructed in 1919. The company is known for its specialty, sugar-coated candy almonds, known as "confetti," which are a traditional treat at Italian weddings. Ferrara's has an extensive market in the Midwest.

Warehouse at 1022 West Taylor Street. This three-story building once served as a storage depot for the Genna brother's bootleg liquor. The warehouse is just four blocks from the Maxwell Street police station, and police could often be seen entering and leaving the locale where they collected their regular bribes to allow the Gennas to continue their operations. The Gennas are remembered as heroes in Little Italy. Not only did they provide good incomes for many of the poor, but architect Tony Genna designed

Sullivan and Wright

Two of Chicago's most renowned architects are Louis Henri Sullivan and Frank Lloyd Wright, both of whom have left a distinctive mark on the city's architecture.

Sullivan's early designs for steel-frame skyscraper construction led to the emergence of those structures as a distinctive American building type. His buildings are admired for their fusion of bold architectural forms with rich ornamentation.

Wright, Sullivan's most famous pupil, is a master of architectural principles. Wright avoids anything that might be called a personal style, but in all his designs, he is guided by what he terms "organic architecture." By this he means that a building should be a dynamic structure and should relate harmoniously to its natural surroundings.

Jane Addams's Hull House holds a place in the hearts of many Chicagoans and is an inspiration for tourists.

a number of low-rent apartment buildings to help supply decent housing to his countrymen.

Hull House, 800 South Halsted Street. Originally a country home owned by Charles J. Hull, this renowned settlement house was established in 1889 by social reformers Jane Addams and Ellen Gates Starr, who recognized the needs of the immigrant poor in the neighborhood. Addams and Starr dedicated their lives to fighting juvenile delinquency, teaching immigrants to speak English and become American citizens, and acting as a welfare agency for needy families. Many Chicagoans still remember the establishment with fondness. "My mother used to press three pennies in my hand and send my sister and me two blocks to the House, where we were showered, cleaned, and sent to an 'open air' room to dry off. Later, we spent our three pennies for a bowl of lentil soup, a bologna sandwich, and a glass of milk,"[9] reminisces one Chicago woman.

The settlement has grown over the years to include twelve brick buildings that cover an entire block. Today, Hull

House is a school, infirmary, cultural center, public bath, gathering place, kitchen, and home-away-from-home for thousands of Chicagoans. Chicago's first public playground, one of its first kindergartens, and one of the nation's first juvenile courts exist on the premises.

Cicero

One of Chicago's most notorious suburbs can be reached by following 22nd Street due west about six miles from Pilsen. Cicero, an industrial town characterized by redbrick buildings, is built for practicality rather than beauty. It is a growing community, however. Many of its residents work at the nearby Western Electric plant making telephones and related equipment.

Most of Cicero's inhabitants are immigrants from eastern Europe, and drinking beer is part of their culture and lifestyle. Thus, gangster Al Capone has found the suburb to be a safe and profitable locale for many of his criminal enterprises. Due to an unspoken agreement between the gangster and city leaders, there are no brothels in Cicero itself, but saloons, gambling halls, and racetracks abound. Refer to the index for descriptions of infamous Cicero locales including Anton's Hotel, the Hawthorne Inn, the Hawthorne Smoke Shop, and the Pony Inn.

Hawthorne Kennel Club, 3301 South Laramie Avenue, Cicero. Dog racing is illegal in Illinois, but due to Capone's influence, greyhounds race on the club's half-mile track, breaking from a line of eight kennels at the starting gate, then reaching speeds of forty miles an hour as they sprint after a mechanical rabbit. The club is a favorite of Capone, who loves to gamble. For those who might like to test their luck, be aware that dog racing is an unregulated sport and fixed races make winning unlikely.

Hawthorne Park Race Course, 3501 South Laramie Avenue, Cicero. Hawthorne Park is a horse racing facility, complete with viewing stands, a restaurant, and dozens of beautiful thoroughbreds. Keep your eyes open if you go—the course is another favorite of Capone, who loves to bet on horses as well as dogs.

CHAPTER FOUR

Other Things to See and Do

Whether it's beautiful scenery or imposing architecture, historic locales or sports venues, Chicago has it all. Weather and the seasons will affect what you choose to do and see, of course, but everyone from eight to eighty will find something of interest among the city's numerous attractions and activities.

Lake Michigan

Lake Michigan is one of Chicago's most impressive features, and many of the city's outdoor pleasures are linked to its shoreline. There are twenty miles of lakefront, much of it sandy beach, so those who enjoy boating, sailing, swimming, or sunning will not be disappointed if they venture down to the water. The months May through October are the best time for outdoor activities. Winter excursions to the shore can be cold and windy, but those who brave the elements will find Lake Michigan an awe-inspiring example of nature's grandeur even in the rain or snow.

Harbors

Chicago's lakefront has many small coves where boats can be moored. Three harbors are notable for their size, however.

Belmont Harbor. Located north of Lincoln Park, this harbor was the home of the Lincoln Park Yacht Club until it combined with the Chicago Yacht Club in 1920. The latter's barge and clubhouse were set in place in 1921. (The Chicago Yacht Club also has a clubhouse in Chicago Harbor). Mayor William "Big Bill" Thompson, a member of the Chicago Yacht Club, sometimes moors his yacht *Valmore*, in this harbor.

Diversey Harbor. Located at Lincoln Park, this long, thin harbor offers plenty of safe mooring for boats large and small.

Chicago Harbor. Located where the Chicago River and Lake Michigan meet, this roomy harbor is the home of hundreds of ships and boats. It accommodates two yacht clubs: the Chicago Yacht Club, located on Monroe Street, and the Columbia Yacht Club at the end of Randolph Street.

Beaches

Chicago has miles of beaches where residents and visitors can swim. Some locales have swimming jetties, bathhouses, and nearby snack bars. Others are undeveloped. Some of the best and most popular beaches are in or near Lincoln Park. They include Edgewater Beach, Rogers Park Beach, Wilson Avenue Beach (private), and Clarendon Beach.

Clarendon Beach at the end of Clarendon Avenue is Chicago's trendiest swimming locale in the Uptown region. Although the beach itself is barely two blocks long, its attractions are so great that almost two million people visit it annually. The site has a bathhouse that provides lockers for men and women, a child welfare station, and a laundry. Swimsuits and towels are available to rent for ten cents. Lifeguards are on site to prevent drownings and floodlights allow for night swimming. A raised 650-foot-long wooden promenade allows spectators to view the water activities in comfort.

Beachgoers should stake a place on the shores of Lake Michigan early in the day to beat the throngs of people who crowd the area by noon.

Bathing Suit Rules

Those planning to swim in Lake Michigan should be aware of Chicago's official bathing suit rules, published by the Committee on Parks, Playgrounds, and Beaches in a 1916 Annual Report. Although rules have been gradually relaxed to allow for modern attitudes and styles, individuals who wear more abbreviated suits may be subject to arrest or prosecution.

GENERAL—No all white or flesh colored suits permitted, nor suits that expose the chest lower than a line drawn on a level with the arm pits.

LADIES—Blouse and bloomer suits may be worn, with or without skirts, with or without stockings, providing the blouse has one-quarter arm sleeve or close fitting arm holes and providing the bloomers are full and not shorter than four inches above the knee (top of patella). Jersey knit suits [with trunks] may be worn . . . providing the suit has a skirt or skirt effect. . . . The bottom of the skirt must not be shorter than two inches above the bottom of the trunks.

MEN—Men's suits must have skirt effect, or shirt worn outside of trunks, except when flannel knee pants with belt and fly front are worn. The trunks must not be shorter than four inches above the knee (top of patella), and the skirt must not be shorter than two inches above the bottom of the trunks.

Visitors of color take note: Many of Chicago's beaches are restricted to white patrons.

Parks

Chicago is a metropolitan area, but, due to the foresight of city planners, it has many parks. Most are small, but a few are truly notable for their size and variety of attractions. Some are spectacular amusement parks. All are pleasant recreational spaces where visitors can enjoy an afternoon or evening of family entertainment. Again, visitors of color take note that many parks are restricted to Caucasian patrons.

Lincoln Park. This 1,119-acre green space on the North Side of Chicago is the largest of Chicago's parks. It has beaches, small lakes, miles of walking paths, a flower conservatory, a bird sanctuary, and the Lincoln Park Zoo. There are also tennis courts and riding trails within its borders. A bronze statue of Abraham Lincoln, created by Irish American sculptor Augustus Saint-Gaudens, stands near the southern entrance.

Garfield Park. Located in western Chicago, this 187-acre park includes green spaces, two man-made lakes, and the world famous Garfield Park Conservatory.

Lincoln Park Zoo

In 1868, Chicago's Lincoln Park commissioners received a gift of a pair of swans from New York's Central Park commissioners. The birds became popular attractions and marked the beginning of the Lincoln Park Zoo. In 1874, commissioners purchased the first animal for the Lincoln Park Zoo: a bear cub that cost $10.

The building covers 4.5 acres, contains almost a quarter of a million plants and flowers, and is lofty enough for palm trees to reach their full growth.

Riverview Park. Located on Chicago's North Side, this 140-acre park is bounded by the north branch of the Chicago River and Belmont and Western Avenues. Within walking distance of several streetcar lines, it is primarily an amusement park and picnic grounds where visitors can enjoy food, carnival rides, and exhibits at reasonable prices. Adults will appreciate the park's lively music and carefree atmosphere. Children will love the carousel and penny arcades. Young people will flock to the newest roller coasters, which travel at breakneck speeds, and will want to spend an hour or two at the Riverview Roller Rink. One note of caution to picnickers: Prohibition agents have been known to make raids on bootleggers and local residents who come to the park's picnic grounds to sell homebrewed beer. There is no danger involved, however, since guilty parties usually surrender their kegs, and the agents depart leaving patrons to enjoy their evening in peace.

Jackson Park. Located on Lake Michigan between 56th and 67th Streets, Jackson Park was designed by renowned landscape architect Frederick Law Olmsted for the World's Columbian Exposition of 1893. It has gardens, walking paths, lagoons, and a Japanese garden with authentic Japanese statuary. This park also has one of the first public golf courses ever created.

Grant Park. Bounded by Randolph Street, Roosevelt Road, Michigan Avenue, and Lake Michigan, this gem of a park is considered part of Chicago's "grand front yard." Its main points of interest are the Art Institute of Chicago and the Clarence Buckingham Memorial Fountain, which was built in 1927. The fountain is distinguished for its finely wrought bronze sculpture and decorative details.

White City. Located on Chicago's South Side at 63rd Street and South Parkway, this impressive amusement park can be easily accessed from the South Side "L." Impressive at night when its thousands of lights dazzle the eyes, the park offers attractions such as roller coasters, outdoor concerts in sunken gardens, and a landmark Electric Tower. The latter is nearly three hundred feet tall and illuminated by twenty thousand light bulbs. White City's spacious boardwalks allow visitors to stroll, explore the park, and people-watch to their hearts' content.

Union Park. Many Chicago park facilities exclude African Americans, but Union Park administrators encourage use of the park by the growing number of black residents who live due west. The park with its green spaces, athletic fields, and fresh air has become a place where both races can come together. It is located on West Randolph Street.

Historic Locales

O'Leary's Barn, 137 DeKoven Street. Many who visit Chicago want to see the site where the Great Fire of 1871 began. According to long-established accounts, the O'Leary cow kicked over a lantern in the barn, igniting the blaze. Subsequent investigations show, however, that the fire probably was caused by boys smoking in the hayloft.

Although the O'Leary house was not burned, the neighborhood was destroyed and is very different today from what it was in 1871. Nevertheless, interested spectators can revisit the scene and speculate on the truth behind the tragedy.

The Old Chicago Water Tower, 800 North Michigan Avenue. One of the few buildings that survived the Great Fire of 1871, the Old Chicago Water Tower stands as a slender symbol of the past among the more substantial buildings on Michigan Avenue. Designed in Gothic style by architect William W. Boyington, the 154-foot structure with its stone-cut battlements and domed roof was a part of the Chicago water system. The system pulled water from the bottom of Lake Michigan, sent it down sloping tunnels to a pumping station, then pumped it to the top of the tower. From there, pressurized water was distributed to municipal water mains (pipes). The tower still houses the 138-foot vertical standpipe, which was

Form and function mesh in the prominent, impressive water tower on Michigan Avenue.

used to equalize the pressure of the water, pumped from the pumping station to the mains.

The Wrigley Building, 400 North Michigan Avenue. Headquarters of the world's leading manufacturer of chewing gum, the Wrigley building is well worth a look, especially at night when floodlights illuminate its white terra cotta exterior. The building, completed in 1924, is modeled on the Giralda Tower of the cathedral in Sevilla, Spain, and is one of the earliest skyscrapers built in Chicago. Its wedding-cake embellishments and clock tower make it an extraordinary sight at any time.

The Rookery building will stand the test of time, its structural integrity assured by its steel frame.

The Tribune Tower, 435 North Michigan Avenue. Home of the *Chicago Tribune* newspaper, the Tribune Tower was constructed in accordance with a winning design in an international competition held by the paper in 1922. It is modeled on the Butter Tower of Rouen Cathedral in France, but its Gothic revival design was modified to accommodate modern skyscraper styles. The façade of the tower is inset with stones from famous buildings throughout the world including Westminster Abbey (England), the Alamo (Texas), the Taj Mahal (India), the Great Pyramid (Egypt), and the Arc de Triomphe (France).

The Rookery, 209 South LaSalle Street. Named for the rooks (crow-like birds) that once nested here, as well as for Chicago politicians who were in the habit of "rooking" (swindling) the public, this massive office building was built in 1885 using modern steel-frame construction and masonry. The bird motif is incorporated into its exterior design. Inside, note the white marble stairway in the enormous lobby as well as the custom light fixtures in the glass-roofed atrium. Architect Frank Lloyd Wright renovated both the lobby and atrium in 1907.

Public Libraries

Chicago Public Library, Michigan Avenue between Washington and Randolph

A Library Rises from the Ashes

The total destruction of the city in the Great Fire of 1871 led directly to the establishment of Chicago's Free Public Library. As money and supplies poured into Chicago, Londoner A.H. Burgess devised a plan that came to be known as the "English Book Donation." "I propose that England should present a Free Library to Chicago, to remain there as a mark of sympathy now, and a keepsake and a token of true brotherly kindness forever," he stated. An appeal for donations was sent to British writers, booksellers, and publishers and was printed in the London *Times*. The response was enthusiastic and overwhelming. Private donations included gifts from Queen Victoria, Benjamin Disraeli, Alfred Lord Tennyson, and Robert Browning. In all, over eight thousand titles representing works in the classics, fine arts, theology, philosophy, natural sciences, and English history were sent to Chicago.

Streets. In January 1873, at the urging of leading citizens of Chicago, the city council established the Chicago Public Library. Its motto was and remains: to inform, educate, delight, entertain, and inspire Chicagoans of all ages, nationalities, ethnic groups, and economic backgrounds.

The first library was a long-abandoned iron water tank at LaSalle and Adams Streets, and contained 3,157 volumes. The collection gained a permanent home in October 1897, when the new central library building opened its doors to the public for the first time. A.H. Coolidge, its designer, kept the Great Fire of 1871 in mind by building the facility to be virtually fireproof.

Coolidge did not focus solely on practicality in his designs, however. At the Washington Street entrance, visitors will see the building's grand staircase. The circulation room has hanging lamps designed by the Tiffany Glass Company of New York. The room's domed ceiling is decorated with inscriptions of sixteenth-century printers' marks, authors' names, and quotations that praise learning and literature. The walls, columns, and arches are inset with mosaics of colored stones, mother-of-pearl, and favrile (iridescent) glass. The base of the dome is inscribed with a quotation from poet, essayist, and playwright Joseph Addison: "Books are the legacies that a great genius leaves to mankind, which are delivered down from generation to generation as presents to the posterity of those who are yet unborn."[10]

Timothy Beach Blackstone Memorial Branch Library, 4904 South Lake Park Avenue. Dedicated in 1904, this first neighborhood branch of the Chicago

The Robie House

One of Frank Lloyd Wright's most popular styles is that of the prairie house, a design that suggests the idea of a long, low structure that hugs the Midwest prairie. One of the finest expressions of this style is the Frederick C. Robie House. The three-story home stands no taller than surrounding two-story houses. On its south façade, fourteen glass doors open onto a main-floor balcony, which shades the ten windows on the ground floor below. A shallow roof overhang allows sunlight to enter through the main-floor doors in winter but keeps sunlight out during the hot summer months. At noon in midsummer, sunlight just reaches the foot of the glass doors, thereby leaving the interior in shade. This design for a hot summer climate illustrates the architect's sensitivity to the environment.

Frank Lloyd Wright points out special features of his Robie House, a design he called "the cornerstone of modern architecture."

Public Library is located in Hyde Park and was named after one of Chicago's leading philanthropists who was also the president of the Chicago Alton Railroad from 1864 until 1899. The building is modeled after the Erechtheum, a Greek temple, and demonstrates the Ionic-Grecian style. It has solid bronze doors and a magnificent rotunda with a dome embellished with decorative panels by Chicago painter Oliver Dennett Grover.

Newberry Library, 60 West Walton Street. For those who are interested in scholarship and research, the Newberry Library, located just west of State Street, is an independent research library that concentrates on the humanities. Free and open to the public, it houses an extensive noncirculating collection of rare books, maps, and manuscripts. Borrowing books requires a library card, but visitors are welcome to browse through reading materials.

The library was founded at the bequest of Walter Loomis Newberry, a businessman and prominent citizen, who was an active book collector, founder of the Young Men's Library Association, and president of the Chicago Historical Society before his death in 1868. The Newberry Library building itself is a notable landmark, known for its striking Romanesque façade.

University of Chicago

The University of Chicago, a thirty-minute train ride south of the Loop, is an essential attraction for anyone who is interested in culture and higher education. The university was founded in 1890 by the American Baptist Education Society and oil magnate John D. Rockefeller and was located on land that was donated by Marshall Field, owner of the Chicago department store that bears his name. The university is not only a leader in higher education and research, it also exhibits striking examples of English Gothic architecture. Its magnificent Rockefeller Memorial Chapel, dedicated in 1928, contains a seventy-two-bell carillon with bells that range from less than eleven pounds to over thirty-seven thousand pounds.

On nearby Woodlawn Avenue, visitors can view stately brick mansions that the university built to provide housing for its professors. Inventor Frederick Robie's unique home, designed by architect Frank Lloyd Wright, can also be seen on Woodlawn. Note the home's linear, geometric form and its exquisite leaded and stained glass doors and windows.

One of the university's more renowned alumni, treasury agent Eliot Ness, has recently begun an attack on Chicago gangster Al Capone's bootlegging industry. Ness earned degrees in business and law, and polished his knowledge of criminology at the university under the guidance of well-known law enforcement expert August Vollmer.

Visitors to the Art Institute of Chicago can explore its galleries for hours and still not see everything the museum has to offer.

Museums

Field Museum of Natural History, 1400 South Lake Shore Drive. Located near Grant Park, and named after Marshall Field who donated $1 million toward its development, the museum was established in 1921. It presents an impressive display of plants, animals, and early people from around the world, some of which were displayed in the World's Columbian Exhibition of 1893.

The museum has a sizable collection of Native American artifacts. Its European collection is relatively small, but is first-rate and well preserved. Objects include fresco paintings, bronzes, and jewelry from the Roman period.

Among the museum's most recent acquisitions are the preserved bodies of the "man-eating lions of Tsavo," which for nine months in 1898–1899 terrorized African and Indian workers who were constructing a railroad bridge in Uganda. After 135 men were killed, the two beasts were shot and killed by Colonel J.H. Patterson, an engineer working on the railway project. The lions were purchased by the museum in 1924.

Art Institute of Chicago, 111 South Michigan Avenue. The art institute was established in 1879 and houses one of the major art collections in the world. It has an outstanding collection of antiquities, classical sculptures, and paintings by Old

Masters such as El Greco, Peter Paul Rubens, and Rembrandt. In 1922, Bertha Palmer, wife of Potter Palmer, also donated her private collection of impressionist art by artists Pierre Auguste Renoir, Edouard Manet, Jean François Millet, and others. Palmer was one of the first Americans to appreciate the impressionists and displayed many pieces of their work in her home until her death in 1918. A more recent collection, presented in 1926 by Frederic Clay Bartlett in memory of his wife Helen, includes many notable post-impressionist paintings. One of the most eye-catching is Georges Seurat's *Sunday on La Grande Jatte.*

The Art Institute, built in Renaissance style, is easy to find on Michigan Avenue due to the large pair of bronze lions that guard its entrance.

Sports Arenas

Sports fans should be sure to visit Chicago's sports arenas, either to take in a game or just to see the facilities. There are several from which to choose, or visit them all.

Wrigley Field, 1060 West Addison Street. Home of the Chicago Cubs baseball team, Wrigley Field was named for Cubs owner, chewing gum magnate William Wrigley Jr. The field was constructed in 1914 and is located on Chicago's North Side. In 1917, the park hosted a classic moment in baseball history with the legendary pitching duel between Jim "Hippo" Vaughn and the Cincinnati Reds' Fred Toney. Both men threw no-hitters for nine innings until Reds outfielder Jim Thorpe (a former Olympic champion) drove in the only run and won the game.

Comiskey Park, 35th Street and Shields Avenue. Also known as White Sox Park, Comiskey Park opened on July 1, 1910, and is named after park owner Charles Comiskey. It features spacious dimensions and was enhanced by a double-decked outfield grandstand in 1927.

White Sox outfielder "Shoeless Joe" Jackson takes a swing during batting practice. Despite the 1919 Black Sox Scandal, baseball fans continue to flock to games at Comiskey Park.

One of Comiskey Park's most famous players was "Shoeless Joe" Jackson, who was involved in the Black Sox Scandal of 1919. Jackson helped the White Sox win the World Series in 1917, but he and six of his teammates were accused of accepting money from gamblers to lose the series two years later. Jackson, who had earned his nickname by once playing a game in his stocking feet, was found not guilty but was banned from professional baseball for life. Many Chicagoans believe that he and his teammates were unjustly accused; others see the case as evidence of Chicago corruption.

Soldier Field, Lake Shore Drive and 16th Street. This sports arena opened in 1924 as a forty-five-thousand-seat municipal stadium in Grant Park. It was created as a memorial to soldiers of World War I and rests on ten thousand pile foundations that were driven through fill material at the edge of Lake Michigan. Views of the city and the lake from the stadium are spectacular.

While the field is primarily used for football games, in 1927 it hosted the Fight of the Century, a professional boxing match between former heavyweight champion Jack Dempsey and challenger Gene Tunney. Ticket sales to the match totaled over $2.5 million and drew such notables as Capone, who reportedly refrained from fixing the fight at the request of Dempsey himself.

CHAPTER FIVE

Notorious Chicagoans and Their Headquarters

The prosperity of the 1920s has not only benefited ordinary Americans. Coupled with Prohibition, it has helped criminals to prosper as well. In Chicago, crooked politicians have enabled mobsters like Al Capone to take control of parts of the city and its suburbs, set up their headquarters in public buildings, and walk the city streets with impunity. While the situation is lamentable, it also provides interested visitors a unique opportunity to see and visit the haunts of some of the most notorious outlaws in the United States.

Restaurants and Bars

Colosimo's Café, 2126 Wabash Avenue. No visit to Chicago would be complete without a look at of the headquarters of James "Big Jim" Colosimo, boss of Chicago's underworld before 1920. Colosimo's Café opened in 1910 and was from the beginning one of the most popular restaurants in the city.

From the street, Colosimo's is a modest two-story brick building wearing its name in block letters across the face. Inside, however, the establishment is ornate. The walls are decorated with green velvet tapestries, gilt mirrors, and Mediterranean murals. The ceiling is painted sky blue and embellished with fluffy clouds and chubby cherubs. Huge crystal and gold chandeliers hang over the tables, which sparkle with glass and silver. The bar is solid mahogany and mirrors.

There are no closing hours at Colosimo's, and patrons from all walks of life enjoy its fine food and imported wines. Opera star Enrico Caruso, stage stars John Barrymore and Al Jolson, and socialites Marshall Field and Potter Palmer often dine in the same room as gangsters named "Izzy the Rat" Buchalsky and "Monkey Face" Genker. Some patrons enjoy dancing and listening to the five-piece orchestra, while others prefer to

Colosimo's Café offers patrons an opportunity to enjoy good food and peruse the site of its owner's violent end.

play dice and card games in the gambling rooms upstairs. Colosimo, now deceased, once had the habit of walking through the establishment during the evening, his large dark mustache bristling, the diamonds in his rings, tie tack, belt buckle, and suspenders sparkling.

Despite its reputation for fun and good entertainment, Colosimo's was the scene of a tragedy in 1920. Colosimo, who specialized in extortion and prostitution and owned about two hundred brothels in and around the city, fell in love with one of the young singers at his restaurant and began neglecting his criminal enterprises. His assistant, John Torrio, tried to persuade him to concentrate on business, especially the growing business of bootlegging, which had the potential of making them multimillionaires.

Colosimo ignored him, to his own detriment. On May 11, 1920, shots rang out in the foyer of Colosimo's. The staff rushed to the scene and found their boss lying on his back, dead. The killer was never found, but everyone knew Torrio had ordered the killing. Torrio took over Colosimo's organization and ran it as he chose for the next six years.

The Four Deuces, 2222 South Wabash Avenue. The Four Deuces, Torrio's former headquarters, is located one block from Colosimo's Café. From the street, the four-story redbrick building looks innocent enough, but inside it is a seedy, run-down den of vice. The first floor is a saloon where bootleg whiskey sells for twenty-five cents a shot. Torrio's office is on the second floor; a gambling den where poker, roulette, and blackjack can be played is on the third; and a cheap brothel is on the top floor.

Those who hope to catch a glimpse of the powerful gangster at the Four Deuces are bound to be disappointed. After his retirement in 1925, Torrio spent several years in Italy and is now a resident of New York City. Those who have seen the man, however, will testify that he does not fit the dark-browed, menacing gangster stereotype. Rather, he is small, pale, and quiet; does not carry a gun, drink, smoke, or swear; and prefers to go home to his wife after a day at the office. Reportedly, he spends his evenings listening to the radio and playing cards.

Although mild at home, Torrio gained a reputation for being brutal when it came to his work. Prostitutes and underlings who tried to double-cross him were beaten or killed. He preferred to negotiate with his enemies, but when necessary he used violence on them as well. Rumor had it that he sometimes ordered them tortured and killed in the basement of the Four Deuces, after which their bodies were carried out a secret tunnel and dumped. No reliable witness actually saw this part of the building, however.

Sieben Brewery

After manufacturing beer became illegal in 1920, the Sieben Brewery at 1464 Larrabee Street was leased out to a businessman who claimed to be a manufacturer of a nonalcoholic brew. In fact, the facilities were controlled by gangsters Dion O'Banion and John Torrio, who continued to oversee the production of an illegal product. A few days after O'Banion sold his share of the brewery to Torrio in May 1924, federal agents raided Sieben's and arrested Torrio for liquor violations. Torrio spent nine months in the Lake County prison in northeastern Illinois as a result.

Visitors to the huge brick structure should note that Sieben's is one of the largest breweries in Chicago.

Mayor William "Decent" Dever padlocked the Four Deuces for a time in 1923, so Torrio quietly moved two blocks away to 2146 South Michigan Avenue, a place of business that Capone maintains today. A plaque on the door reads "A. Brown MD" and the front office is fitted up as a waiting room in a doctor's office. Note that "A. Brown" has long been a favorite alias of Capone. In the back of the building sits the offices of Jack "Greasy Thumb" Guzik, the organization's accountant, who keeps records of Capone's many vice operations.

The Four Deuces' infamous reputation does not stop some brave tourists from trying to get a taste of bootleg alcohol.

People come from all over to snap a picture of Al Capone's home, whose modest exterior disguises luxurious furnishings.

Residences

Torrio's Home, 7011 Clyde Street. Those who want more details of Torrio's life can drive past the tidy, redbrick apartment on Clyde Street that was his home. There, in 1925, three men including gangster George "Bugs" Moran attempted to assassinate Torrio on the sidewalk as he and his wife returned from a shopping trip in the Loop. Torrio was shot in the neck and the groin, but managed to survive and recover. As a result of the attack, he turned his businesses over to Capone, who then became crime boss of Chicago.

Capone's Home, 7244 South Prairie Avenue. An informal tour of Capone's hangouts should begin with his residence on South Prairie Avenue, a street that some of the wealthiest Chicagoans have called home. Meatpacking mogul Philip D. Armour resided at 2115 South Prairie, and two blocks north of the Armour mansion sits the former residence of Marshall Field at 1905 South Prairie.

The Pullman home at 1729 South Prairie is just two blocks north of Field's mansion.

The neighborhood where Capone lives is many blocks south of Chicago's industrialists' mansions, and his home is respectable, but not showy. While the flat-topped, redbrick, two-story structure is modest for such a wealthy man, inside Mae Capone, wife of Al Capone, has furnished it with Chinese rugs, a seven-foot bathtub, marble sinks, and full-length mirrors in the den. Capone's mother, Theresa, has her own apartment of rooms and reportedly delights in cooking for her family, exchanging recipes with other women in the neighborhood, and going to mass at nearby Saint Columbanus Church at 331 East 71st Street.

Anton's Hotel, 4835 22nd Street, Cicero. In 1923, when Mayor Dever's efforts to clean up Chicago made it unprofitable for Torrio to headquarter in the city, he sent Capone to the suburbs to find a new spot to set up operations. Capone chose Cicero on the city's western border. Anton's, an unpretentious brick hotel and restaurant located in the heart of the suburb, became his first headquarters. The establishment was owned by Theodore "Tony the Greek" Anton, a friend of Capone who was murdered by an unknown assailant in 1927. The murder remains unsolved.

Hawthorne Inn, 4823 22nd Street, Cicero. Early in 1924, Capone moved his headquarters down the street from Anton's to the Hawthorne Inn, a three-story brown brick building located one block west of Cicero Avenue. It, too, was owned by Anton. Those who walk past the inn can still see the steel shutters Capone had installed during his term there. His offices occupied one floor of the building.

Bullet scars in the inn's façade are the reminders of an attack on Capone by Hymie Weiss, one of his rivals, on September 20, 1926. Aiming to eliminate Capone and his men, Weiss and several carloads of his men drove slowly down 22nd Street spraying machine gun bullets into the inn and parked cars, shattering window and car glass and splintering wood in the inn and other storefront businesses. Property damage was extensive, but Capone was not hurt in the raid.

Metropole Hotel, 2300 South Michigan Avenue. The Metropole sits in a bustling Chicago neighborhood close to the Loop. Capone lived there from the spring of 1925 to the summer of 1928, paying $1,500 a day to maintain a five-room suite, four guest rooms, a gym complete with rowing machines and punching bags, and several rooms set aside for gambling. His office was located in Room 406, a turret in the corner of the building. There, he sat at a large desk flanked by pictures of George Washington, Abraham Lincoln, and William Hale Thompson, and met with lawyers, judges, and politicians who wanted to ask for favors or cut deals with him.

Chicago Crime Commission

It may seem to many Americans that crime is being allowed to run unchecked in Chicago, but such is not entirely the case. In 1919, a group of thirty-five prominent Chicago businessmen created the Chicago Crime Commission that today serves the greater Chicago area as a nonpartisan, nonprofit organization designed specifically to combat crime.

The crime commission works tirelessly to educate the public about crime-related issues. It reviews and reports on legislation relating to crime, addresses crime problems through programs and services, and tries to ensure the integrity of law enforcement and criminal justice systems. Some wonder if their efforts are making any difference, and the question is justified. Still, at least they are trying.

Members of the Chicago Crime Commission examine guns seized from some of Chicago's bootleggers. The commission works tirelessly to keep the city's streets safe.

Visitors to the luxurious Lexington Hotel might catch a glimpse of Al Capone himself in the lobby.

Lexington Hotel, 22nd Street and Michigan Avenue. The Lexington is Capone's headquarters today, and it is the most lavish of his centers of operation. The hotel's façade combines Moorish and Italian elements and is made up of four towers. Its lobby is tiled in black and white; its elevator is iron-grilled. Capone lives on the top floor with a view of Chicago's South Side. Oriental rugs cover the oak parquet floors in his suite. A chandelier hangs from the high ceiling and an artificial fireplace sits on one wall. Capone's bathroom is outfitted with a huge sunken bathtub with gold-plated faucets and tiles of Nile green and royal purple. At the Lexington, Capone maintains all the added luxuries—gym, gambling rooms, guest rooms, and so on—that he enjoyed at the Metropole. He meets visitors at his large mahogany desk, bedecked with a French telephone, a gold-plated inkstand, and a herd of miniature ivory elephants. On the wall, in addition to the three portraits mentioned earlier, he has three stuffed deer heads, a cuckoo clock, and photographs of his favorite movie stars: comedian Fatty Arbuckle and silent film actress Theda Bara.

Parkway Hotel, 2100 Lincoln Park West. George "Bugs" Moran, one of Capone's most persistent enemies, makes his home in the quiet, secure Parkway Hotel on the western edge of Lincoln Park. Moran's headquarters was originally the Schofield Flower Shop on 738 North State Street (see chapter six), but in 1928, he moved to an undistinguished set of rooms in an office building at 127 North Dearborn. Moran conducted much of his business, however, at the S.M.C. Cartage Warehouse at 2122 North Clark Street (see chapter six). Until recently, the warehouse served as a storage and transfer center for bootleg liquor. The Parkway Hotel and Cartage are within walking distance of each other.

Chicago City Hall, 121 North LaSalle Street. Dedicated in 1911, city hall occupies the west half of an eleven-story building that takes up an entire block of LaSalle. The east half of the building

City Hall

The present city hall is the seventh building formally used for that purpose in the history of Chicago.

The first was the Saloon Building on the southeast corner of Clark and Lake Streets from 1837 to 1842. In 1842, offices were moved to a building owned by Mrs. Nancy Chapman at the corner of LaSalle and Randolph Streets.

In 1848, the Market Building was built on State Street and used as a city hall until 1853. At that time, an official city hall building was constructed on the site of the present city hall, bounded by Clark, Randolph, LaSalle, and Washington Streets. That building was used until the Great Fire of 1871 destroyed it.

After the fire, city business was conducted for a short time at the First Congregational Church at Ann and Washington Streets. Then officials moved to temporary quarters in the West Madison Street police station until 1872. City offices were next established at the Old Rookery Building at Adams and LaSalle Streets until a rebuilt city hall was ready for occupancy. That official building was occupied from 1885 until a gas explosion led to its demolition in 1908. A new—and present—city hall was constructed beginning in 1909 on the same site. The final move was made into that building in February 1911.

houses Cook County offices. The structure is built of gray granite and marked by long colonnades of nine-foot-wide columns. Four relief panels, sculpted in granite, flank the main entrance on LaSalle. They illustrate four features of municipal government: city playgrounds, public schools, the park system, and the water supply system. Inside the entrance, to either side of the marble stairway, are bronze tablets showing former city halls from 1837 to the present.

One of the most colorful and controversial tenants of city hall in 1929 is Mayor William "Big Bill" Thompson. Born in Boston, Massachusetts, he was a cowboy in Wyoming and Nebraska in the 1880s before he moved to Chicago to enter politics in the 1900s. After serving as a Second Ward alderman (representative), he ran for mayor in 1915 and won.

Chicagoans have learned that Thompson is flamboyant and entertaining, but he also changes his position on political issues to serve his own interests. At different times, for instance, he has been pro- and anti-Prohibition. He first promised to make Chicago the most lawful city in the world, then championed a "wide open" town—that is, one where laws regulating prostitution, gambling, liquor sales, and so on are not enforced.

Chicagoans grew tired of Thompson in 1923. Not only had he offended many by being pro-German during World War I, he was also being investigated for fraud by the state's attorney. Rather than run for reelection and lose, Thompson left town for a time, and William Dever, a reform

Pineapple Primary

Al Capone's involvement in the April 1928 Republican primary made that election one of the most violent of the twentieth century. Capone supported Mayor William "Big Bill" Thompson's choices for various offices; Capone's rival "Diamond Joe" Esposito, however, backed another set of candidates. To eliminate the opposition, the two gang leaders launched a series of assaults on the candidates, their supporters, and each other. The attacks were characterized by the widespread use of bombs nicknamed "pineapples."

Chicago police seemed incapable of stopping the violence, which finally claimed the life of Esposito himself. Chicago clergymen finally united to make a joint statement denouncing the violent tactics: "Ours is a government of bombs and bums. . . . O Lord! Grant that we may be awakened to a sense of public shame."

Democrat, was elected mayor. By 1927, however, Thompson had returned and when he ran for mayor again, he won. Gangsters like Capone, who contributed millions to Thompson's campaign, at least partially explain his success.

Visitors to city hall may get a chance to see the mayor, but not Capone, who in the past liked to stroll back and forth in front of the building, greeting his friends and making the point that he is a hard-working businessman. Capone has been keeping a less public profile as of late, due to the crackdown on crime following the St. Valentine's Day Massacre (see chapter six). In addition, he and his family like to spend time at their Miami, Florida, estate, which Capone purchased in 1928.

CHAPTER SIX

"Must See" Murder Sites

Chicago has been the site of much gangland violence during the Roaring Twenties, and the locales of some of the most notorious killings are included in this chapter. Some visitors might be offended at the thought of visiting scenes of murder and death, judging it too morbid a vacation pastime, while others will find such locales interesting and even historical. After all, few other cities in America have the reputation for sheltering murderers like Al Capone, for tolerating gun battles in the streets, and for being entertained by gangster funerals that rival parades.

Popular Businesses

Colosimo's Café, 2126 Wabash Avenue. Site of the murder of James "Big Jim" Colosimo in 1921 (see pp. 55–57).

Schofield Flower Shop, 738 North State Street. State Street is one of Chicago's main thoroughfares, and the Schofield Flower Shop is easy to find for those who stroll down the 700 block. From all appearances, the business is like any other, with its name spelled out in graceful script above a canvas awning on the façade. Those who step inside will appreciate the spacious showroom, full of plants, ferns, and flowers. The shop has long been the headquarters of North Side gangsters, however, and on November 10, 1924, it was the unlikely site of the assassination of gang leader Dion O'Banion.

O'Banion, an Irish immigrant with a love of flowers and a ready handshake, always carried a gun and had been known to kill a man for the slightest insult. An unpredictable ally, he had recently double-crossed John Torrio and Capone in a business deal and undoubtedly was gloating as he worked in his shop on the morning of November 10, preparing flower orders for an upcoming funeral.

Sometime in midmorning, three well-dressed men entered the shop. O'Banion stepped forward to greet them, probably thinking they had come to place an order. As he stuck out his hand, however, one of the newcomers grasped his wrist tightly while the other two pulled out guns. Six shots rang out, and when O'Banion's assistant ran to see what had happened, he found the shop empty and his employer lying dead in a pool of blood. The police made no arrests in the case, but rumors alleged that the killers were hit men hired by Torrio and Capone to avenge the double-cross.

Schofield Flower Shop customers can purchase gorgeous arrangements on the spot where gangster owner Dion O'Banion was assassinated.

Sbabardo's Funeral Parlor, 738 North Wells Street. This decorous building is owned and run by John A. Sbabardo, a mortician preferred by Chicago gangsters who appreciate his skill at making up the bullet-marked bodies of victims so they appear natural during their funerals. Among those corpses prepared by Sbabardo were O'Banion's and Capone rival Hymie Weiss's.

O'Banion's funeral attracted some ten thousand mourners and interested spectators who gathered at Sbabardo's and walked in a procession that extended for a mile and included three bands and a police escort. More than two dozen cars carried flowers (purchased at Schofield's Flower Shop) from the funeral home to the Mt. Carmel Cemetery where O'Banion was buried.

In addition to being a gangland undertaker, Sbabardo is a municipal judge, elected in 1926. Because of his gangland involvement, both his business and his home were bombed during the violent Pineapple Primary of February 1928. The funeral home still bears the scars of that attack.

Street Sites

Site of the Death of Frank Capone, 22nd Street, Cicero. In April 1924, mayoral elections were held in Cicero, and Capone ordered his men to cruise the streets, harassing voters and making sure they voted for his corrupt candidate. There were incidents of violent behavior throughout the day: One election clerk was kidnapped, a policeman was assaulted, and four people were killed.

Because of the violence, several plainclothes police in unmarked cars were called in from Chicago to help keep order. Near dusk, as they neared a Cicero polling place, they recognized Capone's older brother Frank—also a gangster—who acted as a link between his brother and business owners in the suburb. As the officers got out of their cars, Frank came toward them, apparently reaching for his gun. The police began shooting, and when they stopped, Frank lay dead on the street.

Capone was grief-stricken and spared no expense when it came to his brother's funeral. It was one of the grandest the city of Chicago had ever seen. Frank's

Al's Big Brother

Some experts in law enforcement believe that Frank Capone, Al Capone's older brother, could have been even more notorious than his brother if he had lived. Although he was tall, handsome, polished, and made a good first impression, he was more inclined to use violence than Al was. When he uttered his favorite phrase, "You never get no back talk from a corpse," in his quiet, ominous voice, listeners took notice and took care.

Hundreds of mourners line Angelo Genna's funeral procession. The damaged lamppost that Genna crashed into can still be seen at the corner of Ogden and Hudson Avenues.

coffin was silver plated and satin lined and lay in state at the Capone home. Memorial flowers spilled out over the front porch and festooned the lampposts. The crowd of mourners in the funeral procession stretched for blocks. The *Chicago Tribune* reported, "Dressed in their best, bringing their womenfolk, . . . the kings, princes, nobility, and commonality of the underworld gathered in hundreds yesterday to pay their past respects to their late brother in arms, Frank Caponi [Capone]."[11]

Angelo Genna's Assassination Site, Ogden and Hudson Avenues. On the morning of May 25, 1925, Angelo "Bloody Angelo" Genna, one of the fierce Genna brothers who were rivals of Capone, left his home in his new $6,000 roadster. He had $11,000 in his pocket to pay for a house that he and his new wife were planning to buy in the suburb of Oak Park. At the intersection of Ogden and Hudson Avenues, four men in a sedan pulled up beside him and began firing at him with shotguns. Genna floored the gas pedal and led a chase down Ogden, firing back at his attackers as he drove. At a turn, however, he lost control of his car and crashed into a lamppost. While he lay stunned, his assassins pulled along side and shot him repeatedly.

Genna was taken to Evangelical Deaconess Hospital with a severed spine, and died there a short time later. The police guessed that three of the killers were Hymie Weiss, George "Bugs" Moran, and Vincent "The Schemer" Drucci, who killed Genna in retaliation for O'Banion's murder the previous autumn.

Genna's funeral procession included three hundred automobiles and $25,000 worth of flowers. In a bizarre twist, his shotgun-blasted roadster, draped in black, was towed along. Among the mourners were a state senator, two state representatives, and Capone.

The Tommy Gun

Murder became easier in the 1920s with the advent of the Thompson submachine gun, named after its inventor Brigadier General John T. Thompson. Invented to be used by the military in World War I, the gun came into the hands of gangsters after the war and has become a status symbol as well as an ideal weapon of offense and defense.

Known as the "tommy gun," "chopper," "typewriter," or "Chicago typewriter," the gun is light enough to be easily carried and can fire a thousand cartridges per minute. In December 1926, *Collier's* magazine called it "an infernal machine," and judged that it was "the diabolical acme [peak] of human ingenuity in man's effort to devise a mechanical contrivance [means] with which to murder his neighbor."

Church Site

Holy Name Cathedral, State Street and Superior Street. With its beautiful rose windows and graceful spire, Holy Name Cathedral is well known as the cathedral of the Roman Catholic archdiocese (jurisdiction of the Archbishop) of Chicago since 1874. Built of limestone and designed in simple late Victorian Gothic style, it is one of the stateliest cathedrals in the city.

Capone's rival Hymie Weiss was a devout Catholic and called Holy Name his home church. On October 11, 1926, however, the cathedral became a silent witness to his murder, as Capone's hit men took revenge for Weiss's attack on the Hawthorne Inn the month before. In that earlier incident, Capone had narrowly escaped death.

Capone is well known for the success of his retaliations, and this incident was no exception. As Weiss and four associates got out of cars and began to cross the street to the Schofield Flower Shop, machine gun fire and shotgun blasts issued from a second-story window above their heads. Weiss was hit ten times and died almost instantly. The men who accompanied him were wounded and tried to duck around the corner of Holy Name, which faced the flower shop, but machine gun fire followed them and finished them off. Some of the flying bullets also chipped letters from the inscription on the cornerstone of the cathedral, which originally read: "At the name of Jesus every knee should bow in Heaven and on Earth." Those who visit the cathedral today will find the inscription reads: "Every knee should in Heaven and Earth."

When police investigated the second-floor room from which the attack had come, they found empty machine gun cartridges and shotgun shells, hundreds of cigarette butts, and a gray hat bearing a label from a shop near the Hawthorne Inn in Cicero. The evidence pointed to Capone, but once again, the gangster was never arrested.

Massacre Site

S.M.C. Cartage Warehouse, 2122 North Clark Street. Site of the St. Valentine's Day Massacre, this dingy warehouse on Clark Street is fast becoming one of the most notorious and oft-visited spots in Chicago. Squeezed between two three-story rooming houses, it is a one-story terra cotta brick garage with its windows painted black to prevent the curious from peering inside. A large placard bearing the name "S.M.C. Cartage" sits in the window, and

The Chicago garage where members of Bugs Moran's gang were gunned down attracts many curious visitors.

the words "moving" and "expressing" are printed on either side of the door, implying that Cartage is a furniture hauling company.

In fact, Cartage served as Moran's main liquor warehouse until early this year (1929). Moran, a rival of Capone, has repeatedly tried to kill him and his men. By early this year, Capone had had enough. He gave the okay to "Machine Gun" Jack McGurn, one of his closest associates, to eliminate Moran.

McGurn staged his attack for St. Valentine's Day. On the morning of February 14, 1929, seven members of Moran's gang arrived at the garage to inspect a liquor shipment. A few minutes later another car pulled up outside. Four men, two of them dressed as police, got out and entered the garage. When Moran's men saw the uniformed newcomers, they laid down their guns, and faced the wall. With their backs turned, they could not see McGurn's men produce submachine guns from under their coats and open fire. A few minutes later, their mangled bodies lay sprawled in pools of blood on the cement floor. Ironically, Moran was late to the meeting and thus escaped assassination.

Those who visit the warehouse today should turn and look before entering to see the rooming houses across the street at 2119 and 2125. From the upper windows, the killers looked out to survey the garage while planning the murders. Those visitors who enter the garage itself will be able to see vestiges of the victims' blood, not only on the floor, but also spattered on the brick wall at the rear of the building.

Murderous Dr. Mudgett

Chicago in the 1920s does not have a monopoly on murder. In the 1880s, Dr. Herman Mudgett, alias Henry H. Holmes, embarked on a life of swindling, torture, and murder that makes Al Capone look like an amateur. After graduating from the University of Michigan Medical School, Mudgett bought a row of connected three-story buildings at 63rd and Wallace Streets, and turned them into a grand hotel called "The Castle." There, unknown to anyone, he equipped the second floor with devices of torture and murder. A chute led to the basement, which was set up with quicklime pits and a furnace to dispose of bodies.

The doctor was believed to have done away with hundreds of men, women, and children, although only thirty were identified. His motives were greed as well as a sadistic love of killing. He was finally hanged on May 7, 1896, for a murder he committed in Philadelphia, Pennsylvania.

Hotel Site

The Pony Inn, 5613 West Roosevelt Road, Cicero. The Pony Inn is a shabby brick speakeasy east of Austin Boulevard, and the sidewalk outside its doors was a scene of death on April 27, 1926. The victim in the incident was twenty-six-year-old William McSwiggin, a well-liked assistant state's attorney from Chicago. Nicknamed the "hanging prosecutor," McSwiggin was a hard worker with a reputation for winning difficult cases. Despite his reputation, however, he was a longtime friend of brothers Myles and William "Klondike" O'Donnell, gangsters who were rivals of Capone.

On the night of April 27, McSwiggin went out with Myles O'Donnell and some friends to find a card game they could join. Late that evening, however, Capone learned that the O'Donnell car had been spotted in his territory. Since the brothers had lately been trying to take over some of his bootleg liquor operations, Capone considered this an act of provocation. Determined to teach his rivals a lesson, he and his men piled into several cars and sped off in search of the trespassers.

Capone soon came across O'Donnell and several others in front of the Pony Inn. He and his men opened fire, not realizing that McSwiggin was a part of the group. Caught in a spray of machine gun bullets, the attorney and a gangster named Jim Doherty were killed instantly. Everyone knew that Capone was guilty of the crime, but he was never arrested for the murders. The incident exposed the deep and pervasive links between Capone and the powers at city hall.

Grave Sites

Mt. Carmel Cemetery, Harrison and Hillside Avenues. There are many fine cemeteries worthy of exploration in Chicago, but visitors who want to see the gravesites of the most infamous gangsters of the 1920s should go to Mt. Carmel.

Located across the street from the Queen of Heaven Cemetery, Mt. Carmel is the oldest Catholic cemetery in the western part of the Archdiocese of Chicago. Those who scan its headstones will realize that the vast majority of persons interred are of Italian ancestry.

Dion O'Banion. O'Banion's grave was originally in unconsecrated ground because Cardinal George J. Mundelein refused to allow a notorious criminal to be buried among good Catholics. Five months after his death, however, O'Banion's wife quietly moved his remains to one of the most prestigious parts of the cemetery. A granite shaft that reads "My Sweetheart" marks the site.

William McSwiggin. Not far from O'Banion's grave is the burial spot of McSwiggin, who died in Capone's attack on the O'Donnell brothers. Visitors will have to look carefully to find the plain, solid tombstone that marks McSwiggin's grave.

Hymie Weiss. A miniature chapel topped with a sturdy cross marks the

Oak Wood Cemetery

This notable South Side cemetery, located at 1035 East 67th Street, is not far from Lake Michigan. It is the resting place of James "Big Jim" Colosimo, who was killed by an unknown assailant on May 11, 1920.

Colosimo's funeral services were held at his home on 23rd Street, after which a procession of five thousand friends, associates, and onlookers marched through town to the cemetery. As the cortege passed Colosimo's Café, two brass bands played from their station at the front of the building. Mourners included nine aldermen, three judges, two congressmen, a state senator, an assistant state's attorney, and numerous criminals.

The gangster's remains rest in a small granite mausoleum, topped by a cross, and identified by the name "Colosimo."

burial spot of Weiss, whose real name was Earl Wajciechowski.

Vincent "The Schemer" Drucci. One of O'Banion's thugs, Drucci earned his nickname because of his imaginative but impractical robbery and kidnapping plans. He engaged in several daredevil gunfights with Capone's mob, and was arrested on April 5, 1927, for planning election day terrorism against opponents of Mayor William "Big Bill" Thompson. In a police squad car on the way to headquarters, however, Drucci tried to take a gun away from an officer and was shot dead.

Drucci's real name was DeAmbrosio, so visitors should look for a granite mausoleum with that name above the entrance.

Angelo, Mike, and Anthony Genna. Another gray stone mausoleum marks the family burial plot of the Genna brothers. On June 13, 1925, less than one month after Angelo's assassination, Mike "The Devil" Genna was killed by police after he staged an unsuccessful ambush on Moran and Drucci. On July 8, Anthony "Tony the Gentleman" Genna was killed by an unknown assailant. Some suspected that Drucci was the killer. The three brothers were assassinated within forty-two days of each other, and their passing marked the end of the Genna gang.

CHAPTER SEVEN

Shopping in the City

Ever since 1858, when entrepreneur Potter Palmer began greeting his customers at the door of his small dry goods store, remembering their tastes, and displaying Parisian gloves and Belgian glass for them to purchase, shopping in Chicago has been a unique and delightful experience. Palmer not only treated his patrons like valued guests, he offered them free delivery and the option to buy goods "on approval" (that is, after inspection at home). The new policies became so popular that Macy's in New York City and other large stores across the country and in Europe soon adopted them.

Those who step through the doors of Chicago's luxury department stores today will not only be dazzled by their size and splendor, they will also find that Palmer's policies are still in practice. For those who are more comfortable shopping in a slightly less magnificent setting, however, the city has many large discount stores that provide value, quality, and a wide range of choices. And for anyone who simply wants to pick up a can of tooth powder or a pair of socks, there are a multitude of small neighborhood shops where employees are friendly and helpful. Hotel management is happy to advise you where to make your purchases.

Luxury Stores

Marshall Field and Company, State and Washington Streets. One of the city's oldest and most prestigious businesses, Marshall Field and Company occupies an entire city block and is eleven stories tall. Dry goods mogul Marshall Field, once an employee of Potter Palmer, purchased Palmer's Dry Goods on Lake Street and moved it to the present location in 1868, rebuilt it after the Great Fire of 1871, and then expanded it between 1900 and 1907 to its present size and grandeur. The store's neoclassical design is unique for a department store. Its front façade on State Street is ornamented by four marble Ionic columns and gives an impression of authority and reliability commonly seen only on the façades of banks and government institutions. A well-mannered doorman stationed at the main entrance politely escorts customers—often the city's wealthiest and most elite—inside.

First-time visitors to Marshall Field should be prepared to take time to admire the store's many amenities and look at merchandise that ranges from baby buggies to fur coats. Note that store aisles are wide and displays are set up for comfort and modesty when one reaches for an item. For those ladies wishing to purchase intimate items, female salesclerks are available in those departments. Credit and layaway plans are also available.

Marshall Field has much to offer in addition to fine service and merchandise. Fashion shows and cooking demonstrations are just some of the in-store attractions. The store has several restaurants and elegantly furnished men's and women's lounges where customers can rest or socialize. There are also facilities where customers can send and receive telegrams, arrange hotel reservations, purchase theater tickets, consult railroad timetables, and obtain other helpful information regarding travel and the city.

Carson Pirie Scott, State and Madison Streets. Another celebrated downtown business, Carson Pirie Scott was originally constructed in 1899 to be the Schlesinger and Meyer Department Store. Schlesinger and Meyer, however, was purchased shortly after its completion in 1904 by the already prosperous Carson Pirie Scott and Company. Today, the store offers the same variety, quality, and deluxe service as its competitor, Marshall Field and Company.

For those who appreciate unique architectural design, the exterior of Carson Pirie Scott warrants close examination. Its front façade, designed by American architect Louis Henri Sullivan, is an intricate and decorative cast-iron piece. The outside walls of the first two floors reflect Sullivan's taste for ornamentation, while the remaining twelve floors above are a contrast in simplicity, with geometric windows evenly spaced within a structural steel skeleton.

The Boston Store, Madison Street between State and Dearborn Streets. Occupying half a block on the north side of Madison Street, the Boston Store is seventeen stories tall and has twenty acres of floor space. Its features, which many believe make it a worthy competitor of Marshall Field and Company, include a post office, a Western Union office, a bank, a barber shop, a first-aid station, several soda fountains and restaurants, and an observation tower 325 feet above street level. According to a sales brochure, it was the first State Street store with escalators.

The building houses several small factories, which manufacture goods such as ice cream and cigars that are sold in the store. It also has chemical laboratories for testing products and a staffed children's playroom. Its employees enjoy lunchrooms, private reading rooms, and a full-size tennis court on the roof.

Popular Alternatives

The Fair, Adams Street between State and Dearborn Streets. The Fair is an eleven-story Chicago landmark whose owner, E.M. Lehmann, is dedicated to serving aspiring middle- and working-class people. He stocks and sells attractive but lower-priced furniture, household, and personal items. Lehmann is also responsible

The Carson Pirie Scott department store can be appreciated inside and out. It offers an excellent clothing selection and features an intricate, eye-catching façade.

for publishing the first full-page department store advertisement in the city's history, and his sixteen-page Christmas advertisements have proven eye-catching and persuasive.

Loren Miller, Broadway and Lawrence Avenue. The leading department store in the Uptown district is named for its founder, one of the most prominent businessmen in the city. The building's neoclassical style makes it highly visible on Broadway, and its large show windows entice customers in by showing off the latest fashions and unbeatable bargains. The store specializes in selling to middle-class homemakers who appreciate its proximity, variety of merchandise, bargain pricing, superior customer service, and liberal credit policies.

Mandel Brothers, State and Madison Streets. Brothers Simon and Leon Mandel established their store in 1855, moving it to its present location on State Street in 1874. The store is a huge, thriving enterprise that sells a variety of goods ranging from lace and linens to smoking jackets, postcard albums, and dolls.

North American Building, State and Monroe Streets. This nineteen-story structure, notable because of its white terra cotta exterior, was built in 1912. Unlike many of the other elaborate buildings that house department stores on State Street, the North American Building devotes its first twelve stories to small retail shops of all descriptions. Be sure to allow adequate time to browse.

South Center Department Store, 421 East 47th Street. The three-story South Center Department Store opened in 1928 as one of the largest retail establishments on the city's South Side. On opening day, the *Chicago Defender* wrote, "Hundreds of persons crowded the store to scrutinize the wares. With fifty different departments, everything is carried that is sold by the finest Loop stores."[12]

The Legacy of Molly Netcher

Charles Netcher, who began his career as a bundle wrapper and cash boy in the Partridge dry goods house, founded the Boston Store shortly after the Great Fire of 1871. He chose the name as a marketing strategy, hoping that Boston's strong reputation in merchandising would help his own dry goods establishment. Apparently it did, because the store expanded rapidly.

Netcher was not the only force behind the Boston Store's success, however. In 1891, he married one of his clerks, a young woman named Mollie Alpiner. After her husband died in 1904, Mollie went on to transform the old-fashioned dry goods store into the first-rate, full-line department store it is today.

The South Center is more than a store known for its variety of merchandise, helpful service, and reliability. It welcomes the presence of thousands of south Chicago blacks who live in the area, offering them everything from hats and handbags to candy and canaries. Store management also has a policy of hiring as many blacks as possible, providing them well-paying jobs as well as valuable experience in retail merchandising. The policy is designed to boost the economy of the neighborhood as well as help modify Chicago's discriminatory hiring practices when it comes to persons of color.

Discount and Chain Stores

H.C. Struve Company/Goldblatts, 3155 North Lincoln Avenue. H.C. Struve is the largest department store in the Lincoln-Belmont retail and entertainment district, an area that is convenient to transit connections. Many North Side and suburban residents enjoy shopping in this area rather than making a longer trip to the Loop. While Struve's lacks the glamour of Marshall Field's, it can be relied on to carry the clothing and household goods that are popular with the average homemaker.

As of this year (1929), Struve's is being taken over by the Goldblatt's chain of discount department stores. Expect the store to maintain its tradition of reasonable prices and helpful service. Other Goldblatt's stores are located at 1615 West Chicago Avenue, 47th Street and Ashland Avenue, and 91st Street and Commercial Avenue.

W.A. Wieboldt Company, Milwaukee Avenue near Ashland Avenue. Wieboldt's is a chain of midsize, neighborhood-oriented department stores. German American W.A. Wieboldt established his first small shop in 1884 on Milwaukee Avenue, the heart of Chicago's ethnic, working-class West Side. Today, he continues to cater to the needs of ordinary, working-class people and is rarely seen in so-called high society. Wieboldt's is able to offer reasonable prices by purchasing in bulk for its four stores and passing the savings on to its customers.

Other Wieboldts are located on Lincoln and School Avenues, Ashland Avenue and Monroe Street, and at Davis and Benson Streets in the northern suburb of Evanston. A fifth Wieboldt's is slated to open in the Englewood district in late 1930.

F.W. Woolworth Company, 219 South State Street and other locales. Known as a "five-and-dime" store, Woolworth's specializes in the sale of everyday household and personal items at bargain prices. It has over sixty stores in Chicago, most of them concentrated in the Loop and in the city's middle-class neighborhoods and business districts. More than just a chain store, Woolworth's has become a part of Chicago's social life. A growing number of young people like to visit with friends over an ice cream soda at a Woolworth lunch counter.

Sears, Roebuck and Company, Homan Avenue and Arthington Street. Most Americans have thumbed through a Sears, Roebuck catalog. A trip to Chicago gives

The traveler on a budget will find plenty to buy at Woolworth's and can take a break from shopping at the lunch counter.

you the opportunity to visit the first Sears retail store in the nation. Located at its huge mail order plant in west Chicago, the store, which opened in 1925, is now one of over three hundred Sears retail stores throughout the country, and features the same variety, high quality, and reasonable prices as does the catalog. In addition to selling merchandise over the counter, the store also has an optical shop and a soda fountain. For those who have become loyal to Sears brands—Craftsman and Kenmore—this is the perfect opportunity to make a purchase.

The Sears site is slightly out of the way, but well worth a visit. Described by Richard Sears as a "city within a city,"[13] the complex cost $5 million to build and covers almost a million square feet of floor space. It includes offices, the mail order plant, and the retail store. There is also a powerhouse and a printing building where catalogs are printed. A prominent clock tower with an observation deck towers above the grounds. Railroad tracks on-site allow an average of two hundred railroad cars to be filled with merchandise and depart the complex every day.

Walgreen Drug Stores, 41 South State Street, 151 North State Street, and other locales. Founded by Charles Rudolph Walgreen in 1901, the Walgreen chain of pharmacies has one hundred outlets in Chicago. They are recognizable for their eye-catching window displays and are growing famous for their soda fountain counter. Even if you don't need anything in the pharmaceutical line, drop in for one of their double-rich chocolate malted milk shakes. Be prepared to stand in line, however, because Chicagoans know how good they are, too.

Ethnic Markets

Chinatown, 22nd Street and Wentworth Avenue. For visitors who want to experience something out of the ordinary, a visit to Chinatown should be a part of their trip. This small but colorful community was created in the 1870s after Chinese immigrants who came to the West Coast to help build the transcontinental railroad began to disperse into the midwestern and eastern United States. By 1890, there were almost six hundred Chinese in the city.

The first Chinese community was built around Van Buren and Clark Streets. Due to tensions between China and the United States, however, prejudice against the newcomers arose. Landlords raised the rent of houses occupied by Chinese so that most could not afford to pay. About half of the entire Chinese population in Chicago was forced to move south to its

Catalog King

In 1886, Richard W. Sears, a railway station agent in North Redwood, Minnesota, purchased a shipment of watches and sold them at a profit to other station agents. Encouraged by his success, he soon quit the railroad, moved to Minneapolis, Minnesota, and formed the R.W. Sears Watch Company. In 1887, Sears moved to Chicago and hired Alvah Roebuck to repair his watches.

In 1893, the two men became partners and founded Sears, Roebuck, a mail order company that sold a variety of products such as clothes, jewelry, furniture, and other household goods. They advertised by means of a catalog and targeted farmers and other rural customers who had limited access to traditional stores. The catalog soon came to be a familiar resource in virtually every home throughout the country.

present location, formerly an Italian and Croatian neighborhood.

A visit to Chinatown today is a chance to experience some exotic and unusual sights and smells. Enjoy a multitude of fresh produce markets, have lunch in a restaurant, or memorialize your visit with an inexpensive souvenir.

The Ghetto, Halsted, Taylor, and Twelfth Streets. Despite the unpleasant associations attached to its name, Chicago's Ghetto is a bustling, upwardly mobile lo-

Shoppers will find great deals and plenty of merchandise at the Maxwell Street Market.

cale, home to thousands of newly arrived immigrants, the majority of them Jewish. Here, small shop owners and street vendors make their living and celebrate their culture as they assimilate into American life. Note the storefront signs lettered in Hebrew and the traditional clothing of some of the salespeople. Enjoy the music, food specialties, and local characters that make the neighborhood unique.

Maxwell Street Market should be an essential part of your explorations in the Ghetto. Officially established in 1912, it is an inexpensive place to buy almost anything: clothing, copper kettles, coffins, bicycle parts, even jinx-removing incense that is guaranteed to improve bad luck. The Jewish Sabbath is Saturday, so the best time to visit the market is Sunday, when most business is conducted. Try bargaining, as merchants expect it. Be prepared for high-pressure tactics, however, especially the "puller," someone stationed in front of a store who can literally drag you inside to shop. Their motto is: "The customer is always held right."[14]

Chicago Nightlife

Chicago offers some of the most exciting nightlife in the nation. Whether you're looking for a fine symphony or hot (exciting) jazz, the latest movie or a glass of bootleg whiskey, you can find something to suit your taste. Remember, however, if you're visiting nightspots some distance from your hotel, it's wise to take a cab or some other reliable form of public transportation. Some neighborhoods can be unsafe after dark, and automobile drivers who have been drinking can be a hazard to other vehicles or to unwary persons crossing the streets.

Opera

Opera is a long, respected tradition in Chicago. The Chicago Opera Association, now known as the Chicago Civic Opera Company, gave its first performance on November 3, 1910, in the Auditorium Building, at 430 South Michigan Avenue. Today, opera enthusiasts still enjoy some of the greatest operatic performances in the world in the Auditorium's exclusive environment.

The Auditorium Building, which also houses a hotel, banquet hall, and offices, is another demonstration of architect Louis Henri Sullivan's talent. Note particularly the triple-arch entrance on Michigan Avenue and the lobby with its marble mosaic floors, hand-stenciled ceiling, and grand staircase. The showpiece of the building, however, is the theater itself, which has long been considered the largest and finest in the country.

Those who attend the opera beginning in November 1929 will be able to enjoy fine performances in a new facility, the Civic Opera House on Wacker Drive along the river. The building is the vision of utility mogul Samuel Insull, a Chicago billionaire known as "the Prince of Electricity." Insull is also the president of the city's opera association.

The opera house is a majestic limestone skyscraper, shaped like a gigantic throne. Designed and decorated in a hybrid of art nouveau and art deco styles, the building's colonnaded portico (covered porch) runs the length of the building on the Wacker Drive side. At the south end, large bronze doors open onto the grand foyer. Inside, Austrian crystal chandeliers throw light on the foyer's gilt decorations and stenciled ceilings. The spacious sweep of floor is covered with pink and gray Tennessee marble. Forty-foot columns are topped with carved

The Civic Opera House is multifunctional; the auditorium is on the first floor and offices tower above it.

capitals covered in gold leaf. An imposing grand double staircase leads to the mezzanine foyer. Don't be afraid that you will be unable to get tickets for a performance at this beautiful new venue because the new opera house will seat over thirty-five hundred attendees.

Symphony

The Chicago Symphony Orchestra made its debut on October 16, 1891, and since December 1904 makes its home in the Theodore Thomas Orchestra Hall at 220 South Michigan. The hall is a red-brick building in neo-Georgian style. It features an auditorium and a high-ceilinged ballroom that is used for receptions and chamber concerts.

Frederick Stock, who was appointed in 1905, is the symphony's music director. Under his direction, numerous renowned performers have been showcased at the hall over the years. For instance, in February 1925, composer-conductor Igor Stravinsky made his debut with the orchestra conducting his *Song of the Volga Boatmen*, *Scherzo Fantastique*, *Song of the Nightingale*, and *Firebird Suite*. In January 1928, composer-conductor Maurice Ravel made an appearance conducting his own *Le tombeau de Couperin*, excerpts from *Daphnis and Chloe*, *Shéhérazade*, *La Valse*, and his arrangement of Claude Debussy's *Sarabande* and *Dance*. In March 1928, twenty-three-year-old pianist Vladimir Horowitz made his debut with the orchestra, performing Sergey Rachmaninoff's third piano concerto.

For those who prefer something less intellectual, the orchestra gives nontra-

A Visit from the President

The Chicago Auditorium opened on December 9, 1889, with renowned operatic star Adeline Patti singing "Home, Sweet Home," to an audience that included President Benjamin Harrison. Harrison took part in the building's dedication and expressed the feelings of many when he stated:

It is my wish, and may it be the wish of all, that this great building may continue to be to all your population that which it should be—an edifice opening its doors from night to night, calling your people here away from the care of business to those enjoyments, and pursuits, and entertainments which develop the souls of men, which will have power to inspire those whose lives are heavy with daily toil, and in its magnificent and enchanting presence lift them for a time out of these dull things into those higher things where men should live.

ditional concerts as well. Children's concerts were initiated in January 1919. In November 1924, the orchestra gave a series of popular concerts at the Union Stock Yards. In February 1926, during a program of African American spirituals, actor, singer, and civil rights activist Paul Robeson made an appearance.

Loop Theaters

Some of Chicago's premier movie theaters are located in the Loop. In them, patrons can watch newly released motion pictures, vaudeville shows, and musical presentations, while enjoying elegant furnishings and satisfying their yearning for culture and refinement. Lines can be long and shows have been known to sell out at times, however, so it is always wise to arrive early to get tickets.

Chicago Theater, State Street between Randolph and Lake Streets. Opened in 1921, the $4 million Chicago Theater was the first Chicago "dream palace," so-called because its size, glamour, and entertainment were able to transport audiences to a world of make-believe. The Chicago is designed along the lines of a seventeenth-century European palace. Its lobby is decorated with marble columns, glass chandeliers, and a red-carpeted stairway to upper balconies. The auditorium's five thousand upholstered seats sit beneath an elaborately sculptured ceiling.

Audiences can expect more than comfort and great movies at the Chicago. The management regularly books dance troupes, beauty pageants, comedy routines, and jazz bands to accompany the feature film. An evening there is definitely worth the price of a ticket.

Oriental Theater, Randolph Street between State and Dearborn Streets. The Oriental Theater has earned a reputation among Chicagoans as one of the best places to enjoy great movies and live jazz bands. Bandleader Paul Ash, known as the "Rajah of Jazz," has been delighting his fans there since 1926. The auditorium holds 3,250 patrons, and its lavish interior is loosely inspired by Indian culture, with bright colors and exotic decorations. The *Chicago Evening American* noted at the time of the theater's opening in May 1926, "No description of the new house can be kept matter of fact. It is an exotic play palace that makes the 'Arabian Nights' wonders come true."[15]

Orpheum Theatre, State Street near Monroe Street. Located in the heart of the Loop, the Orpheum was originally a small vaudeville theater with only seven hundred seats in its auditorium. Today, it is solely a movie house, although it sometimes features popular sing-along slide shows. The theater's entryway with its bright electric lights is designed to catch the passersby's attention. Once inside, auditorium seats are plush and roomy, and the air conditioning system is state of the art. Customer service is valued at the Orpheum as well. Its management makes a point of being polite and courteous at all times.

A top priority for every traveler should be a visit to the Chicago Theater. Its size, beauty, and entertainment will amaze all theatergoers.

Randolph Theater, northwest corner of State and Randolph Streets. The fifteen-hundred-seat Randolph Theater has no stage because it is designed solely for showing motion pictures. It is a no-frills movie house, showing second-run films that have been seen earlier at other theaters. Despite that, it does good business on the so-called turnaway crowd—moviegoers who have failed to get into sold-out shows in other theaters.

The Randolph is also unique because it regularly shows movies such as westerns, war pictures, and high adventure films designed to attract a male audience. Note that the management is happy to sell blocks of tickets (sometimes at discounted prices) to special groups such as Boy Scouts or war veterans.

United Artists Theater, southeast corner of Randolph and Dearborn Streets. The United Artists Theater (originally the Apollo) is owned by United Artists Corporation, a motion-picture production and distribution company formed by Hollywood stars Mary Pickford, Douglas Fairbanks, Charlie Chaplin, and Gloria Swanson (a native of Chicago). The theater is the debut outlet in Chicago for all United Artist releases.

Moviegoers can cool off on a hot summer day inside the comfortable Orpheum Theatre.

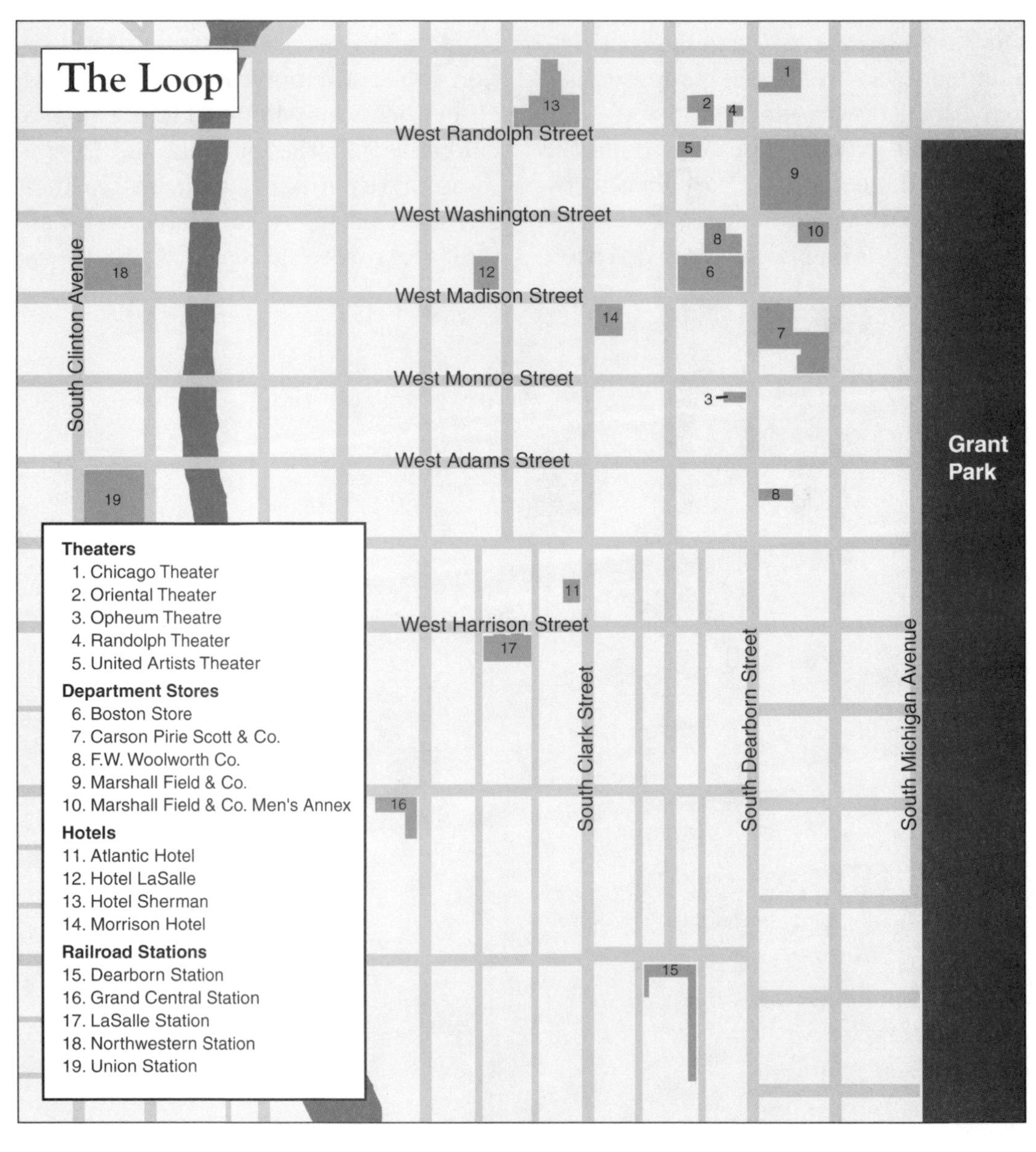

It's easy to find the theater, because its managers promote new films with eye-catching displays out front. At times, banners are hung across the intersection to announce a new release. Attendees will enjoy the theater's Moorish-inspired (North African) style. The lobby features black marble columns and murals depicting scenes from northern Africa. Be sure to notice the auditorium's elaborate gold leafed, domed ceiling.

Neighborhood Theaters

There are too many neighborhood theaters to be listed in any guidebook, but many are comparable in size and luxury to those in the Loop. A few of the best are included here.

Uptown Theater, Lawrence Avenue and Broadway. The Uptown Theater is one of the most spectacular structures on Chicago's North Side, able to seat five thousand people in its grand auditorium. Built in 1925 and decorated in an elaborate Spanish Renaissance style, it has a five-story grand lobby complete with chandeliers, the most expensive Wurlitzer grand organ ever built, and a state-of-the-art air conditioning system. If you have extra time, make the effort to visit the Uptown. It must be seen to be fully appreciated.

Deluxe Theater, 1141 West Wilson Avenue. Also located in the growing Uptown district, the Deluxe is known for its elegant décor as well as its comfortable seating. The lobby walls are lined with marble, and a large pipe organ, once used to accompany silent pictures, is an eye-catcher. In the words of a visiting theater manager, "If the house fails at pictures, it could be readily changed into a church."[16]

Regal Theater, 4719 South Parkway. Set in a predominately African American neighborhood, the Regal combines Spanish, Moorish, and Eastern architectural styles to make a distinctive and glamorous interior design. Its ceiling is draped with a blue-fringed canopy held up by huge poles of gold, and the stage is set within the outline of an Oriental pagoda. Patrons compare the effect to a garden on a moonlit night. While enjoying the décor, the audience can sit in perfect comfort thanks to the theater's air conditioning system. A top-flight stage orchestra often supplements the regular house orchestra.

The Regal is unique from other large Chicago theaters in that its audience as well as its staff—management, house musicians, janitors, and doormen—are African American. Because of that and its setting, the theater is a major institutional presence among black Chicagoans. Parties and philanthropic community events are often held here.

Tivoli Theater, 63rd Street and Cottage Grove Avenue. Just steps away from the South Side "L" and two streetcar lines, the Tivoli—described in 1928 by the *Chicago Evening American* as "a stately white and gold French creation"[17]—is easy to access. Its interior décor is elegant and conservative, reflecting styles popular during the reign of King Louis XIV. At the same time, its modern air conditioning system gives the audience a pleasant break from summer heat. Another point in the Tivoli's favor is the fact that the management does not tolerate noisy, disruptive behavior. A large number of uniformed, highly trained ushers ensure decorum so that the audience can enjoy the show to the fullest.

Music and Dance

Dancing is extremely popular in Chicago, and there are dozens of dance facilities across the city. They vary from small halls to large ballrooms and dance pavilions. Many can be found in hotels and amusement parks. Although some Chicagoans are concerned that such facilities may encourage rude and immoral behavior, a great many others insist that they are simply enjoyable places to spend an evening.

Aragon Ballroom, Winthrop and Lawrence Avenues. Located in the Uptown entertainment district, the Aragon opened in 1926 to thousands of dancers who continue to patronize it today. The ballroom's interior is designed to astonish and impress. A thickly carpeted broad staircase, flanked by large plaster statues, leads to the second-level dance floor. The auditorium is designed to resemble the courtyard of a Moorish castle. Palm trees and twinkling lights in the ceiling add to the feeling of a night under a Spanish sky. The dance floor rides on a cushion of cork, felt, and springs for maximum comfort during dancing.

Be aware that high standards of dress and behavior are the rule at the Aragon.

A Night at the Aragon

This flowery advertisement in the Chicago Evening American *on July 15, 1926, as cited by Scott A. Newman in "Aragon Ballroom," did not exaggerate when it alerted readers to the wonders in store for them at the new Aragon Ballroom.*

The lure of treasures, exotic and opulent [luxurious], whispers from every nook and corner of the new Aragon, enticing dance lovers from the ballroom floor to the discovery of endless new delights. Rare tapestries, bizarre Chinese plates, statuettes, orange trees astonishingly real in the simulation of tropical verdure [greenery], appointments breathing the spirit of Castilian [Spanish] grandeur. Here is the flaming beauty, the romantic glory of old Spain.

Close to $2,000,000 was expended to make the Aragon the most magnificent institution of its kind in the world. . . . Every facility to insure the complete comfort of dance lovers will be found at the Aragon. Commodious checkrooms for both men and women, a handsomely appointed grande mirror salon for the convenience of milady [ladies], a clean wholesome refectory where appetizing refreshments are served by charming señoritas, carefully selected attendants who are guided in their contact with visitors by the creed, "Every patron an honored guest"; these are but a few of the myriad attractive features you will find at the Aragon.

Men are required to wear jackets and ties, and women semiformal eveningwear. Smoking is prohibited on the dance floor, and close dancing or jitterbugging is forbidden. Despite the restrictions, a night at the Aragon is worth your while, and the ballroom's closeness to the "L" makes transportation fast and easy.

Arcadia Ballroom, Broadway and Montrose Avenue. Another popular Uptown ballroom, the Arcadia is famous for its fine jazz bands. Young people in particular enjoy the chance to show off their dancing skills in front of their friends. At times, impromptu dance contests are held, and on select nights the Arcadia hosts roller skating in place of dancing.

Paradise Ballroom, Madison Street and Crawford Avenue. For those on the West Side who want a "proper" evening of dancing, the Paradise Ballroom is the best choice. Patrons are allowed to dance sedate waltzes and two-steps, but not the sprightly fox trot or the boisterous Charleston. Despite these restrictions, the Paradise is extremely popular, perhaps because its dance floor can accommodate four thousand dancers. Another plus is its location, as it is close to the Madison and Lake Streets "L" stops.

Savoy Ballroom, 4733 South Parkway. One of the most lavish ballrooms in the city, the Savoy lies in the predominately African American sector of south Chicago. Most of its patrons are black, but growing numbers of whites visit the Savoy to dance to some of the great music of the day, including Charles Elgar's and Clarence Black's bands. The establishment does everything it can to please its patrons, too, as the *Chicago Defender* noted in 1927:

> Every modern convenience is provided. In addition to a house physician and a professional nurse for illness or accident, there is an ideal lounging room for ladies and gentlemen, luxuriously furnished . . . [and] an ultra modern checking room which accommodates 6,000 hats and coats individually hung so that if one comes in with his or her coat crushed or wrinkled it is in better condition when leaving.[18]

Jazz is hot at the Savoy, and two bands perform every night to permit continuous dancing. Roller skating nights are regularly scheduled at the ballroom as well. Because the Savoy has facilities to hold over four thousand persons, it doubles as a community center and sports venue for black Chicagoans.

Trianon Ballroom, Cottage Grove Avenue and East 62nd Street. Another conservative dance locale, the Trianon is as elegant as it is enjoyable. Its King Louis XVI-style décor, Grand Salon, and spacious dance floor are just a few of its features. Floor men and matronly hostesses circulate among the crowd to ensure that polite behavior is maintained. Women patrons are not allowed to smoke, and there is no "spooning" or

The Arcadia and Savoy ballrooms are popular locations for dancers to show off their Charleston skills.

"petting" between dances. Although black jazz bands are not hired at the Trianon, some of the best white musicians including Paul Whiteman, saxophonist Isham Jones, and Dell Lampe and their orchestras perform here. The Trianon is publicized as a "palace for the people," but patrons should take note that it has a reputation for racial exclusivity. That is, it is open to whites only.

Speakeasies and Jazz

Chicago is home to over a thousand speakeasies of various size and styles.

Chicago Jazz

A new kind of music—jazz—has come of age in black nightclubs around the country. Originating in New Orleans, jazz is characterized by a sense of energy and a melody that does not always follow the beat. Above all, jazz involves improvising. Great jazz players create melody and variations according to their mood and use written music only as a guide for what they feel like playing. For instance, when a new pianist for Joe "King" Oliver's Creole Jazz Band asked for copies of the music the band played, they politely told her they didn't have any. Oliver advised, "When you hear two knocks, just start playing."

Serious mainstream composers now realize that jazz is an impressive new art form and have begun creating jazz melodies of their own. One of the best known is George Gershwin, whose jazz concerto "Rhapsody in Blue" premiered in New York City in 1924, which kicked off his now flourishing career.

Joe "King" Oliver's Creole Jazz Band, featuring the talented Louis Armstrong (standing, center), can be heard nightly at the Plantation Café on East 35th Street.

They are illegal and unregulated, but also lively and fun. In addition, many of them feature the best black jazz bands in the country. Visitors must remember that purchasing alcohol is a violation of U.S. law and that speakeasies are liable to be shut down and padlocked at times. That said, for those who want an exciting night out, a list of a few of the best speakeasies and jazz hotspots follows.

Buyer Beware!

Industrial alcohol—grain alcohol produced for use in the manufacture of rayon, antifreeze, shaving cream, photographic film, and so on—accounts for much of the liquor sold in America today. It originally contains bad-tasting or poisonous substances such as soap, sulphuric acid, or wood alcohol, which have been added during production specifically to prevent people from trying to drink it. Bootleggers—those who illegally manufacture, sell, and/or smuggle alcohol—find it relatively easy to remove the contaminants, however, by "cooking" or redistilling. They then mix the pure alcohol with flavors, additives, or even a little good liquor to give it an authentic taste and appearance. Glycerin and oil of juniper produce an approximation of gin known as "bathtub gin" (so called because water used in making it was often drawn from a bathtub tap). Caramel, prune juice, and creosote make Scotch whisky. While good liquor can take years to make and age, the hallmark of a bootleg operation is speed.

Federal agents pose next to a seized still. Bootleg alcohol remains popular, doctored to remove its unsavory flavors.

Sunset Café, 315 East 35th Street. The café has a modest façade, but it is one of Chicago's legendary jazz spots and a hangout of Al Capone. Its house orchestra has featured such famed musicians as Earl "Fatha" Hines and Louis Armstrong.

Plantation Café, 338 East 35th Street. Across the street from the Sunset Café, the Plantation Café is another top jazz nightspot. It features the legendary Joe "King" Oliver and the Dixie Syncopators.

Green Mill Gardens, 4802 North Broadway. A nightspot that features outdoor dancing and entertainment in a sunken garden, the Green Mill is well known for its gangster clientele. It is a favorite of Capone, who insists on hearing the song "Rhapsody in Blue" whenever he enters the building. Rumors say that "Machine Gun" Jack McGurn owns 25 percent of the facility.

Halligan Bar, 2274 North Lincoln Avenue. Halligan's can be recognized by its triangular shape and is reportedly owned and operated by George "Bugs" Moran.

John Barleycorn, 658 West Belden Avenue. Visitors may walk past John Barleycorn thinking it is an abandoned building. Check with the Chinese laundry in the back, however, and you'll learn otherwise. Reports have it that liquor is transported to the basement in carts owned by the laundry and that drinks are brought up to the pub via a small elevator.

Pony Inn, 5613 West Roosevelt Road, Cicero. Owned by Harry Madigan, the Pony Inn is a two-story white brick building a mile north of the Hawthorne Inn. The Pony offers a place for regulars to drink and gamble. Those who are looking for a thrill can stop and view the sidewalk out front where assistant state's attorney William McSwiggin was shot and killed by Capone's men.

Hawthorne Smoke Shop, 22nd Street, Cicero. Managed by Frank Pope, a Capone hireling, this hard-to-miss red-brick building next door to the Hawthorne Inn offers a full menu of drinks, plus off-track horse race betting, roulette, craps, blackjack, and so on.

Cotton Club, 5342 22nd Street, Cicero. This speakeasy and nightclub, controlled by Ralph Capone, features some of the finest jazz musicians in the nation. The club, characterized by the Chicago Crime Commission as a "'whoopee' spot,"[19] is a favorite of Capone, Mayor William "Big Bill" Thompson, the police, and various unnamed politicians.

Notes

Introduction: Heart of the Midwest

1. Quoted in John Kobler, *Capone: The Life and World of Al Capone*. New York: G.P. Putman's Sons, 1971, p. 221.
2. Lloyd Lewis and Henry Justin Smith, *Chicago: The History of Its Reputation*. New York: Harcourt, Brace, 1929, pp. xi–xii.

Chapter One: A Brief History of Chicago

3. Quoted in "History of the Chicago Public Library," *Chicago Public Library*, www.chipublib.org.
4. Quoted in Robert Cromie, *A Short History of Chicago*. San Francisco, CA: Lexikos, 1984, p. 75.
5. Quoted in Cromie, *A Short History of Chicago*, p. 96.
6. Quoted in Laurence Bergreen, *Capone: The Man and His Era*. New York: Simon and Schuster, 1994, p. 262.

Chapter Two: Preparing for a Visit

7. Quoted in Donald L. Miller, *City of the Century: The Epic of Chicago and the Making of America*. New York: Simon and Schuster, 1996, p. 182.
8. Quoted in "The Great Chicago Fire and the Web of Memory," *Chicago Historical Society and the Trustees of Northwestern University, 1966*. www.chicagohs.org.

Chapter Three: Chicago Neighborhoods

9. Quoted in Robert G. Spinney, *Big Shoulders: A History of Chicago*. DeKalb: Northern Illinois University Press, 2000, p. 158.

Chapter Four: Other Things to See and Do

10. Quoted in "History of the Chicago Public Library."

Chapter Six: "Must See" Murder Sites

11. Quoted in Bergreen, *Capone*, p. 110.

Chapter Seven: Shopping in the City

12. Quoted in Scott A. Newman, ed., "South Center Department Store," in *Jazz Age Chicago: Urban Leisure from 1893 to 1934*, 2000. www.suba.com.
13. Quoted in "The Sears West Chicago Headquarters Building," *Sears Retirees' Site*, 2001. www.retirees sears.com.
14. Quoted in "Maxwell Street Marketing," *Virtual Jewish Chicago*, 1996. www.vjc.org.

Chapter Eight: Chicago Nightlife

15. "Opening of Big Loop House Only Week Away," *Chicago Evening American*, May 1, 1926, p. 13, quoted in Scott A. Newman, ed., *Jazz Age Chicago: Urban Leisure from 1893 to 1934*, 2000.
16. Quoted in Scott A. Newman, ed., "Deluxe Theater," *Jazz Age Chicago: Urban Leisure from 1893 to 1934*, 2000.
17. Quoted in Scott A. Newman, ed., "Paradise Theater," *Jazz Age Chicago: Urban Leisure from 1893 to 1934*, 1998.
18. Quoted in Scott A. Newman, ed., "Savoy Ballroom," *Jazz Age Chicago: Urban Leisure from 1893 to 1934*, 2000.
19. Quoted in Bergreen, *Capone*, pp. 98–99.

For Further Reading

Fon W. Boardman Jr., *America and the Jazz Age: A History of the 1920s*. New York: Henry Z. Walck, 1968. A very good account of the Roaring Twenties.

Martin Hintz, *Farewell, John Barleycorn: Prohibition in the United States*. Minneapolis: Lerner, 1996. Prohibition and its consequences in the United States.

David C. King, *Capone and the Roaring Twenties*. Woodbridge, CT: Blackbirch Press, 1999. Overview of Al Capone's life and events that marked the 1920s, including heroes of the age, the Scopes trial, revival of the Ku Klux Klan, and others.

Edmund Lindop, *Dazzling Twenties*. New York: Franklin Watts, 1970. Good overview of the 1920s. Good pictures.

David Pietrusza, *The Roaring Twenties*. San Diego, CA: Lucent Books, 1998. An examination of all aspects of the 1920s, including Prohibition, presidential scandals, fads, controversies, and the stock market crash. Includes many good primary and secondary source quotes.

Works Consulted

Books

Laurence Bergreen, *Capone: The Man and His Era*. New York: Simon and Schuster, 1994. A well-written, entertaining work focusing on Al Capone and America of the early 1900s.

Robert Cromie, *A Short History of Chicago*. San Francisco, CA: Lexikos, 1984. An award-winning journalist and author traces Chicago's history from its frontier beginnings to the present day.

John Kobler, *Capone: The Life and World of Al Capone*. New York: G.P. Putman's Sons, 1971. Another excellent biography of Al Capone.

Lloyd Lewis and Henry Justin Smith, *Chicago: The History of Its Reputation*. New York: Harcourt, Brace, 1929. A history of Chicago compiled by two leading authors of the 1920s.

Donald L. Miller, *City of the Century: The Epic of Chicago and the Making of America*. New York: Simon and Schuster, 1996. A comprehensive history of Chicago, emphasizing its standing as a great American city.

Geoffrey Perrett, *America in the Twenties: A History*. New York: Simon and Schuster, 1982. An in-depth look at the 1920s. Worth reading.

Robert G. Spinney, *Big Shoulders: A History of Chicago*. DeKalb: Northern Illinois University Press, 2000. A brief, readable history of Chicago.

Internet Sources

"Deluxe Theater," Scott A. Newman, ed. *Jazz Age Chicago: Urban Leisure from 1893 to 1934*, 2002. www.suba.com. Background on the Deluxe Theater which opened in Chicago's Uptown district in 1913.

"The Great Chicago Fire and the Web of Memory," *Chicago Historical Society and the Trustees of Northwestern University*, 1996. www.chicagohs.org. More information on the 1871 fire that changed Chicago history.

"History of the Chicago Public Library," *Chicago Public Library*, 1994–2002. www.chipublib.org. A brief history of a Chicago institution.

"Maxwell Street Marketing," *Virtual Jewish Chicago*, 2000. www.vjc.org. Article describing a popular and historical outdoor market in Chicago's "ghetto" district.

"Opening of Big Loop House Only Week Away," *Chicago Evening American*, May 1, 1926, in Scott A. Newman, "Movie Theater Archives," *Jazz Age Chicago: Urban Leisure from 1893 to 1934*, 2002. www.suba.com. Details the opening of the lavish Oriental Theater in Chicago's Loop in May 1926.

"Paradise Theater," in Scott A. Newman, ed., *Jazz Age Chicago: Urban Leisure from 1893 to 1934*, 2002. www.suba.com. History of the Paradise Theater on Chicago's West Side.

"Savoy Ballroom," in Scott A. Newman, ed., *Jazz Age Chicago: Urban Leisure from 1893 to 1934*, 2002. www.suba.com. Overview of one of Chicago's top night spots in the 1920s.

"The Sears West Chicago Headquarters Building," *Sears Retirees' Site*, 2001. www.retireessears.com. Covers the history of Sears from its beginning in 1896 to the present.

"South Center Department Store," in Scott A. Newman, ed., *Jazz Age Chicago: Urban Leisure from 1893 to 1934*, 2002. www.suba.com. Details the successful opening of one of the largest retail establishments patronized by blacks on Chicago's South Side.

Website

Chicago Historical Society and the Trustees of Northwestern University (www.chicagohs.org). The site includes a wide range of topics relating to the 1920s.

Index

Picture Credits

Cover photo: © Underwood & Underwood/CORBIS
Associated Press, The Journal Gazette, 35
© Bettmann/CORBIS, 50, 52, 53, 61, 67, 77, 96
From the collection of John Binder, 31, 56, 58, 59, 62, 69
Courtesy of the Chicago Landmarks Commission, 33, 37, 41, 48
© CORBIS, 44
Jeff DiMatteo, 22, 25, 27, 28, 90
© Hulton/Archive by Getty Images, 10, 17, 19, 20, 26, 71, 80, 82, 85, 94, 95
Scott A. Newman Collection, 88, 89
© Stock Montage, Inc., 13, 14, 29, 38, 39, 47

About the Author

Diane Yancey works as a freelance writer in the Pacific Northwest, where she has lived for over twenty years. She writes nonfiction for middle and high school readers and enjoys traveling and collecting old books. Some of her other books include *Life in the Roaring Twenties* and *Al Capone*.